The FASTING JOURNEY

Sacrifice.

Purpose.

Joy.

Clarity.

PETER R. HOLMES

The FASTING JOURNEY

Sacrifice. Clarity. Purpose. Joy

Calling for an army of fasters
to learn the discipline and power of fasting
and help advance the cause of Christ.

PETER R. HOLMES

Authentic

COLORADO SPRINGS • MILTON KEYNES • HYDERABAD

Authentic Publishing
We welcome your questions and comments.

USA	1820 Jet Stream Drive, Colorado Springs, CO 80921 www.authenticbooks.com
UK	9 Holdom Avenue, Bletchley, Milton Keynes, Bucks, MK1 1QR
	www.authenticmedia.co.uk
India	Logos Bhavan, Medchal Road, Jeedimetla Village, Secunderabad 500 055, A.P.

The Fasting Journey
ISBN-13: 978-1-60657-018-0

Copyright © 2009 by Peter R. Holmes

11 10 09 / 6 5 4 3 2 1

Published in 2009 by Authentic
Cover design: Dan Jamison
Interior design: projectluz.com
Editorial team: Andy Sloan, Kay Larson, Erika Bremer

Printed in the United States of America

DEDICATION

To all those seeking help
and greater Christ-likeness:
may the fasting journey be for you
a highway to Christ and
greater wholeness.

HEALTH WARNING/DISCLAIMER

CONTENTS

ACKNOWLEDGMENTS

Because my fasting journey spans over four decades, a great number of people deserve to be acknowledged and thanked. Without my wife, Mary, who has written a section in this book reflecting on her experiences living with someone who undertakes regular extended fasts, neither this book nor my fasting journey would have been possible. Despite all my eccentricities, she has stood with me over three-plus decades of marriage—a difficult and challenging task on numerous occasions! I am eternally grateful to Mary for her love and commitment to me.

I would also like to thank the many people whom the Lord has led to me over the years. Some have been in great need, while others simply wanted to know Christ better. These people have been my teachers and the main reason I turned to extended fasting. More than just appointments in my datebook the last few decades, their impact upon me has been enormous. As they shared their need I sought to help them in a lay pastoral setting.

Some of those who came to me had intractable problems beyond my experience. Some had undergone years of traditional and alternative medical treatment, professional counseling, and/or pastoral care without receiving the level of wholeness they were seeking. I would turn to the Lord and fast for the way forward, something very few of them were able to do for themselves. At such times, deep in a fast, touching their pain in my own aching body—in some ways entering the death of Christ—I would most of the time find answers enough to move forward with them. I thank these individuals for the privilege of being able to serve them while also learning from them.

I must also thank Susan Williams, my colleague, who carefully read through the draft and made a number of suggestions, based on her own fasting journey as well as her experiences of working with me while I have been fasting.

Thanks must also go to physician Brian McDonogh, general practitioner and nutritionist, for his invaluable input on the health science aspects of fasting.

Finally, I want to thank and praise Christ my Lord for enduring with me all these years and never faltering in His faithfulness to my earnestness.

FOREWORD

This thorough and relevant treatment of the spiritual discipline of fasting by Peter Holmes is a necessary addition to any serious pastoral library. Dealing with a biblical practice that is often misunderstood and tends to be either ignored or abused, Holmes brings a fresh and profound voice of purpose and relevance to the issue of fasting. He deals carefully with the biblical foundations for the practice, and addresses the theological purpose and practical function of fasting for the church and the individual Christian. His survey of the role of Greek philosophical dualism and its effects upon Western theology and culture, such as asceticism, the dualism of body and spirit, and the tendency to view spirituality in a penitential way provides a contrast to a biblical view of fasting as a means of deepening our relationship with God through Christ.

Holmes's presentation of fasting as participation in the sufferings of Christ and in intercession for others is a refreshing change from some of the traditional penitential, meritorious, and works-oriented interpretations of the discipline. He points out that its purpose is to express one's identification with the sufferings of Christ and to become formed more fully into his image, both as persons and as a community of Christ. In his words:

We surrender to the humiliation of fasting to gain more of the presence and purposes of the Kingdom of God in our lives and in the lives of those for whom we may be fasting. . . . The essence of the Atonement is the giving of Christ's life to all those who will accept His sacrifice. It is Christ's death for our life, an act of voluntary love on His part that we can now appropriate for ourselves. In the same way that we accept this sacrifice of Christ we also accept the discipline of fasting. We surrender to it, suffering for a season and thereby choosing to associate with Christ in His surrendered sacrifice.

Perhaps his most significant contribution to pastoral ministry is his portrayal of the varieties of fasting, key practical principles for the spiritual direction of fasting, and the physical implications of the discipline. Growing out of the physical experiences of a lifetime of participating in this discipline, his very perceptive and practical insights on how to maintain one's health during extended fasts and the health benefits of fasting are invaluable. As he draws from his own study and experiences, Holmes presents us with a clear, biblical, experiential guide to this spiritual discipline that is the most valuable pastoral treatment of fasting available to the church and individual Christian today.

R. Larry Shelton, Th.D.
Richard B. Parker Professor of Wesleyan Theology
George Fox Evangelical Seminary
Portland, OR
Author, *Cross and Covenant*

INTRODUCTION

Several years ago I organized the notes I had taken while fasting to make them available for people I knew who were interested in pursuing fasting as a personal or group spiritual discipline. I called the compilation "Fasting: My Personal Journey." For this is what fasting has been for me—a personal journey. But I have come to realize that what the Lord has taught me through my personal journey might also be helpful for a broader range of readers. So this book is a blend of my personal experience and some recommendations for those who may want to include the spiritual discipline of fasting in their relationship with the Lord and in their relationships with other believers.

As the subtitle suggests, this journey of learning to fast includes numerous aspects. Yes, it is a *sacrifice*, and most of the time it brings profound *clarity*. But it must have a *purpose*, and it will bring *joy* in its wake. For what you fast for in the Lord will bear fruit and allow you to move forward in your personal journey, as well as bless those around you. Fasting is one of the main keys to Christ-like spiritual maturity.

My lifetime has been punctuated by periods of fasting, both learning and practicing the discipline. During these seasons I have fasted for a variety of specific purposes, but four key ones have been my main motivation. First, I wanted to know the Lord more intimately; second, I found myself needing understanding to help sick and damaged people; third, I needed to know how to apply this understanding; and fourth, I needed monetary provision in order to be available to them. The second and third purposes have been my righteous obsession since the 1960s, as I have had a lifetime interest in why people cannot find fulfillment in Christ. The journey of learning how to fast—especially how to prepare properly, what to expect, and what to avoid—now forms the contents of this book.

I realize that I am not typical of people who want to learn to fast. Most of my life I have lived by faith, with irregular sources of income. So at various points I have had to fast for financial provision. I have also been involved in running businesses to generate funds for furthering the Kingdom of God and planting churches. This also required fasting. But the most common form of fasting has been to gain knowledge for the people who came to me wanting to find emotional healing from the Lord and deeper intimacy in their relationship with Him.

The growing body of knowledge I have gained over the years has become a kind of intellectual "wholeness database" for helping others. I have focused on gaining a better understanding of how human nature is constructed—and more importantly, some of the ways we get damaged and sick in the first place. By the 1980s, through study, an inquisitive nature, and knowledge that had come, among other ways, through fasting, I was able to help more and more people who came to me.

These people fell into two main categories: those seeking deeper intimacy with Christ and those who were ill—either physically, emotionally, or mentally. If they were beyond my scope at the time, they often became the subject of a fast or, where appropriate, were referred to professional medical care. After years of treatment, some had already fallen out of the health care system. Sometimes I would fast for several individuals at a time. But they were all my teachers; and I was the student, as the Lord mentored me.

Susan was one of those who came to me in great need.[1] I fasted for her often when it was clear we simply did not have the knowledge from the Lord for the next step of her healing. She also fasted from time to time, sometimes to see a breakthrough in her own discipleship journey and sometimes for others and the Lord's wider work. So it is fitting that she has joined me in contributing to this manuscript.

This journey of fasting has led me into a realm of understanding that was quite new to me. I began to see human nature having a spiritual-emotional aspect, just as Scripture portrays it. But I also began to see that our spiritual-emotional nature is where much human damage seems to reside. This helped me see the importance of giving to the Lord our toxic emotions that may have built up from the past.

I also began to see how God's perspective on human sin and baggage was essential for those needing to unravel the damage of their pasts. I don't remember a time when the Lord did not give the necessary knowledge either to me, to the person I was trying to help, or to someone else. The only caveat to this is that the individual seeking help also had to demonstrate to the Lord that he or she was personally worthy of the Lord intervening through our fasting. Having said that, however, such knowledge and its healing didn't always occur in the time frame or man-

---

1   Susan has written about her own journey in *Letting God Heal: From Emotional Illness to Wholeness*, S. B. Williams and P. R. Holmes (Bletchley, UK: Authentic Media, 2004).

ner we were asking or expecting! Some of my other books document these journeys in more detail.[2]

As I thought about writing this book I also began to realize that the value of my experience of fasting has been much wider than my own personal journey or my goals at the time. Therefore the principles that I am outlining may also be helpful in any setting, for any believer or group, and with any Christ-centered goal.

For me fasting has been both a highway to the Lord and a treasure-trove of ideas of how the Lord sees things and how we need to learn while earnestly at His feet. Having based the book on my own personal experience, my intent is to broaden it into a guide for others to learn how to fast. It is my prayer that this will help those of you who are seeking the Lord and/or fasting for whatever you might feel led to ask from the Lord. Although fasting does not succeed if it is, in reality, an ego trip, I have found that there is much God can give us as we practice this discipline.

The Lord has taken me on a journey; and through my intercessory fasting others, as well as myself, have been helped. In rewriting this material for a much wider readership I began to dream about what could happen if others were to pursue the same journey. So you will find woven into this book a clarion call for an army to rise up in every part of the world to help prepare the way for what I and others have called "the generation of the righteous"—the generation that will stand firm and finally fulfill the Great Commission, thereby helping to hasten the return

---

2   Some of the understanding I have gained is illustrated in the principles documented in the testimonies of people I have helped. *Changed Lives: Extraordinary Stories of Ordinary People*, P. R. Holmes and S. B. Williams (Milton Keynes, UK: Authentic, 2005), recounts twelve stories of individuals from our church and ministry. I have explored these issues more academically in my book *Becoming More Human: Exploring the Interface of Spirituality, Discipleship and Therapeutic Faith Community* (Bletchley, Milton Keynes, UK: Paternoster, 2005).

of Christ (Rev. 19:6–8) —when our wonderful Master and Friend will be reunited with both His creation and His Bride.

Maranatha!
Peter R. Holmes
(February 2009)

Part 1

INTRODUCING FASTING

In this part of the book I am going to
introduce you to the idea of fasting
to the Lord, outlining some biblical
foundations together with aspects of my
own personal fasting journey.

MY FASTING JOURNEY

The longest water-only fast I have done was thirty-nine days when I was in my early twenties. It was an "earnestness to know the Lord" kind of fast, as well as a bit of an ego trip. But after thirty-nine days I was so ill that I had to break the fast. God clearly stood in my path, preventing my ego from having the satisfaction of going forty days (like Jesus!). Many similar extended fasts have followed over the last forty-plus years, most done with far more grace and wisdom than that first extended fast. Let me give you some additional background.

When I was fourteen, in 1961, I remember my spiritual mother, Mrs. Cooper, telling me that she was doing a twenty-four-hour fast. I can't remember now why she was doing this, but I know she fasted on occasion. We talked about her fast while I was frying some eggs to put on my beans on toast, a regular favorite of mine, just before the Bible study at their home on Kohat Road, Wimbledon, UK.

I did the fast with her on a school day, and although I cannot recall any benefit at the time I remember taking to the idea and beginning to fast myself on a regular basis after this. Over the next few years I read anything I could find in the Bible about fasting, as well as any Christian books I could afford or borrow.

I began fasting because I wanted to fast. There was a certain appeal in it—not to punish my body or to be masochistic, but because I wanted to know more about the Lord, to draw closer to Him. I had no specific purpose other than that. I was simply doing what Mrs. Cooper had done, and finding out for myself what it was like.

I found fasting to be both easy and extremely hard. It was easy in that I found the discipline of not eating a simple decision—I just stopped eating. I was not that tempted by food after that. Even in those early days I felt good about completing a fast. But fasting was also hard in that I had a body that enjoyed food, so it would protest even before I stopped eating. We do not recognize until we abstain from food that our bodies have a presumption about always getting what they want.

The central purpose in this early fasting journey was my desire to know Christ better. But I also discovered fasting to be a way of "turning up the volume" with both the Lord and the Enemy. I realized that fasting was a last resort. It gave me an additional weapon in the arsenal of being able to engage myself in spiritual reality, while also discovering I could bring about change in both the spiritual and physical worlds.

In 1968, at the age of twenty-one, I entered Moorlands Bible College. A year later I transferred to London Bible College (now London School of Theology) in the West End of London. By this time I was doing a twenty-four-hour water-only fast every Friday. The rest of the week I ate only two meals a day: breakfast and an evening meal. At lunchtime I ate a piece of fruit and did my Canadian Air Force daily fitness plan. I had a favorite grocer on Marylebone High Street that kept me well supplied.

I often accompanied this routine with an hour of prayer on my knees at my bedside in a room I shared with two roommates before I slept each night. I suppose it was inevitable that other students labeled me "Praying Peter." This discipline of fasting and intercession was an important part of my schooling, a way of learning to let God talk to me.

After graduating from Bible college I continued to do modest fasts on a regular basis while living in the Middle East or Europe in the early 1970s. I was a program director on the ship Logos with Operation Mobilisation (OM), a Christian mission. Then I left my position on Logos but remained with OM in the Middle East and Asia. In 1975 I took the job of administrator of a Christian trust in the UK. Through this privately endowed trust I helped start a variety of evangelistic initiatives, including the Greenbelt Festival and the musical "Lonesome Stone." This was followed by helping to launch Care Trust and later Care Campaigns.

It was during this time that I began to see a shift in the reasons for my fasting. As a teenager my needs were simple and met rather easily, and I had not yet been introduced to our need to change the world! But while I was with OM and in my later work I began to use fasting as an extreme form of intercession. It became that extra, heavy gun I brought out of the armory when I needed it. On my spiritual "volume control," it served as the megaphone or bullhorn that expressed my passion.

I now would describe this shift as moving from a "fast to the Lord," where I was focused on my relationship with Him, to "fasting for needs." I had already prayed for a matter and not been able to see a breakthrough; so now, through my fasting, I brought out the big guns. This type of fast allowed me to declare in life-and-death terms how serious I really was about a particular matter. *God, I am putting my life on the line for this—please hear me!* He always did, one way or another.

While working my jobs I continued skipping lunch, unless I had a business lunch. I also began exploring the idea of more extended fasts. I was still single at the time. I did no preparation; I simply stopped eating.

I can remember very little about those days apart from the sparse notes I kept. I know I suffered the withdrawal symptoms of caffeine and other things that were part of my regular diet. And when breaking a fast I would begin just normal eating. Some of these were "absolute fasts" (abstention even from water) and lasted for several days. Looking back, I now cringe at my irresponsibility toward my young body. I will attempt to outline in this book how *you* should do it, not how *I* did it!

This fasting routine, one way or another, has continued as part of my life ever since. And although my prayer time moved to the early morning, the other routines remained in place throughout seasons of fasting. Even today missing a meal is not something I notice, like most people seem to, as anyone traveling with me will testify. My wife, Mary, has learned over many years of traveling with me that she needs to take provisions, as I will not think of it.

The only exception to these routines occurred while I was doing my PhD, when its academic disciplines and my sedentary lifestyle (hours on my backside) caused me to expand into a ball of lard—which I began losing, with a bit of help, after I had given birth to my degree!

Since the early 1980s I have done at least one extended fast most years, and some years more than one. Most of these were water-only fasts lasting from two to five weeks. A typical length was between fourteen and twenty-one days. I have also done four fasts of over thirty days. Since the early 1970s I have kept notes while fasting. At the time these notes were only for my benefit, a record of my journey and what I had learned. But now they have become a prompt for this book.

Fasting in Regard to Personal Issues

I have fasted for several reasons. Some of my fasts have been motivated by more than one reason. But the main idea has been the discipline of my saying to the Lord that I wanted to know Him better. I had to find ways of saying this and of learning how to clear the debris. I always believed I could do something personally toward this goal. I was never passive. I could not accept that it was all God's responsibility and work to come in intimacy to me.

Initially I fasted because I knew I had things wrong with me. After talking with lots of people, I still couldn't find a way of dealing with these things. Numerous individuals helped me define the problems more precisely, but no one was able to give me a step-by-step way of sorting the issues.

Here is an example: I had an unrighteous hate for my father. When I was a child he had been physically and verbally abusive to me on numerous occasions. At age fourteen I had to leave home to stop these beatings. Both my pastor and the social services had gotten involved because I ended up at Nelson Hospital in Merton Park with a cut in my head that needed stitches. I hated my father deeply, but I knew this was wrong.

During a fast while living in Singapore in my early twenties, the Lord said to me, *You treat me just like your father.* I was shocked and devastated. But it was so obvious and so very true; I did hate my father. No wonder I had a hard time with Father God telling me what to do. So with the help of a friend I began to engage the pain. I gave the trauma of the physical abuse to the Lord, together with its anger and rage. This was accompanied by my fasting.

A few weeks later my travel itinerary brought me through London, and Dad offered to pick me up at the airport so I could spend a weekend at home. After passing through customs and immigration I saw my father, standing there smiling at me. I gave him a hug, then moved off with him toward his Triumph Herald in the parking lot. As we walked together I remember looking at him and realizing that he was a complete stranger to me emotionally. I also realized that this was the first time in my life that I did not want to kill him. The anger—the rage, hate, and revenge—was gone. I was free! I could now get on with my life. I could begin to learn what fathering was from Father God. Fasting worked!

By the time I was in my early twenties I had learned that fasting was a means of gaining knowledge from the Lord. It was a way of prioritizing a need that God would then meet. It was my way of saying to the Lord that I was serious about this issue and desperately needed His help. I needed to see the matter from His perspective, to know some of what He saw and what He might do. So the second reason for my fasting was for knowledge. And the insights the Lord gave me for others frequently exposed issues that I had to be willing to deal with in my own life. God takes every opportunity to help us grow in wholeness!

The Benefits of Fasting in My Life

Although this is not necessarily typical for everyone, each fast I have done has been specific. In the early days it was either for getting to know the Lord better or for being able to hear His voice about why this was not happening. But in time, as I sought specific knowledge to help those who asked me for help, my fasting stopped being so much about me. Later my fasts broadened even further, as I sought help from the Lord for things such as financial provision.

As I began writing this book I realized something amazing: I have never had a fast that totally failed. Some saw delays in being answered, while others saw answers as soon as I began fasting (although in honor of the Lord I continued fasting anyway). In other instances I didn't know that an answer had been received when the fast ended, but looking back now I can see that it had.

Along with specific goals, my fasts were also a spiritual discipline. They all added something to my personal character growth and my relationship with Christ. Although fasting is not a good way to lose weight permanently, and none of my fasts were done specifically for that reason, weight loss has always been a beneficial side benefit.

For me fasting has been also a shortcut to knowledge of human need. It has helped me to see what is obstructing a person's wholeness. I have personally found that fasting is one of the ways God brings healing to people's lives. When God gives the knowledge and it is applied, the often-hidden power of the damage is broken. When we come to the Lord in the earnestness of fasting, He is usually faithful in giving us, or others, such insight. This, in turn, will generally lead to remarkable leaps forward in healing and wholeness for the person, providing he or she is obedient in acting upon what the Lord says (see, for example, Exodus 15:26). Part of my ministry has been to help identify and implement the subsequent steps after the knowledge has been given, because people often need to be taught how to apply the new understanding to their lives.

I use the terms "healing" and "wholeness" in a slightly different way than they are most often used. To begin with, I assume that every young convert will need to embark on a journey to become more like Christ. None of us are born Christ-like. We must all learn. So in this book I will be speaking about the release of knowledge that helps each of us move into deeper relationship with Christ. This knowledge can take several forms, as I will illustrate in due course, though pressing the Lord for this knowledge to change is, I believe, our responsibility. Healing and wholeness is the natural outcome of the positive change of becoming more like Christ.

Fasting has taught me that we are all sick from a "disease" called sin, a disease from which we all need some healing. The level of damage varies from person to person, though sometimes the most damaged among us are also the most gifted and anointed. It seems almost as though the Enemy can somehow see into us and discern what level of threat we could become to him long before we ever know. Getting the knowledge to change is essential if we are to recover all that Christ would have us be. So fasting can be a tool that helps us or others move into more of our spiritual gifting and anointing.

Another area of focus for my fasting has been the need for financial provision. Living by faith, my wife and I have been dependent from time to time on unsolicited gifts. Until recently the only time these gifts came through were after times of fasting. God has given me adequate strength and has required this discipline of me. Fasting, for me, has included the spiritual discipline of laboring for money. Over the years Mary and I have needed to trust the Lord for our provision. We see His faithfulness each day. Although I work part-time as a business consultant, the substantial financial shortfall has always been faithfully met by the Lord.

I am not suggesting that my experience will also work for you. Each person must find the best path for him or her, especially in the area of provision. Although this is how the Lord has dealt with me, His provision may come to you in other ways.

Because I have fasted for knowledge for others or financial provision for myself, fasting has been for me a confidential appointment with the Lord. Asking for specific knowledge as to why a person is sick or admitting I am short of money are not things you talk about to the whole congregation. This has meant that apart from my family and closest friends no one has known what I was doing. This becomes awkward when someone offers you lunch, coffee, or a donut or some other sweet. Keeping your fast secret while also honoring others can be difficult, especially in a case like mine in which many of those I work with are unbelievers. Nevertheless, keeping my practice of fasting private has been a great benefit to me, as it has taught me the humility and graciousness of service.

Doing extended fasts while holding down a full-time job poses challenges. It can be an emotional and relational nightmare. In always seeking to appear normal I believe I am following Jesus' words in Scripture that call for an approach with no ostentation (Matthew 6:16–18). But long-term fasting is an incredible battle. Unlike others I have read about,

I have never had the luxury of taking off a month or more of work to do a fast and then to recover. I have always had to keep working, though I do have to slow down. But except for the people close to me no one would have known I was fasting. The benefits of learning how to do this have been enormous for me, and I believe that anyone who has done the same would agree.

The final benefit I want to mention is that I have always had a sense of destiny—a sense that I am writing history, both with the Lord and others. As evidence of this perception, I have hundreds of pages of notes recorded before, during, and after fasts. Some of this makes terrible reading, since my extended fasts have been so tremendously difficult. This is not the experience of everyone who fasts.[1] Each person's journey is unique, and you will discover in time what your own will be.

Personally, I cannot imagine life without the discipline of fasting. It has made me the man I now am: healthier and fitter, more aware of the spiritual and material realities around me. Fasting has given me a deep love for the Lord and His created world, as well as a sense of His pleasure upon my life. But more than any of these is knowing I have done just a little in spurring on the return of Christ—because of what I have learned, what I have given to others from the Lord, and what I can yet accomplish before He calls me home.

In Summary

My journey of fasting might sound a little intimidating. Extended fasting has become a regular part of my life and ministry. But remember, we all have to start somewhere—usually somewhere much more gentle!

---

1   See, for example, Derek Prince, *Shaping History Through Prayer and Fasting* (Fort Lauderdale: Derek Prince Ministries, 1973); Arthur Wallis, *God's Chosen Fast: A Spiritual and Practical Guide to Fasting* (Eastbourne, UK: Kingsway, 1982).

In fact, the subtitle of this book probably reflects a greater balance. My fasting journey has touched on all four aspects: the clear sacrifice, the clarity I so often gained either during or after the fast, the purpose for doing so, and the outcome of joy when the fruit became apparent.

When I began fasting my fasts were simply to know the Lord better, a way of expressing my earnestness to know Him. They focused on my relationship with the Lord, helping to promote a growing maturity in Christ. But over time I also wanted to make a more significant contribution to the Kingdom of God, though in the beginning I had little idea what that meant and how it would be achieved. It was only after gaining more experience that I began to learn how to focus my fasting toward specific needs.

Looking back I can see this subtle shift throughout my teenage years and into my twenties: from seeking the Lord for myself to seeking things from the Lord, from learning deeper intimacy with Him to beginning to carry the needs of others, as well as my own.

Perhaps you are considering your first fast. Don't let my examples put you off. We all learn by starting with small fasts. Fasting is a discipline that we grow into by starting gradually. I will describe in this book how to do this.

On the other hand, you might be preparing for your first extended fast. I have deliberately included my own experience of such fasting in detail in order to enable others to learn safely. I will be very specific about the impact of fasting, providing numerous examples from my own life.

Regardless of how much or little you have practiced the discipline of spiritual fasting, I hope this book will be a valuable resource for you in your own journey.

2.

THE PURPOSE OF FASTING

In every instance fasting has had a positive impact on me and my deepening intimacy with Christ. As you grow in your own fasting journey I would expect you to experience the same. I know of no more effective way of growing in your relationship with God and in your capacity both to stand with Him and to serve Him.

Fasting has been a key spiritual discipline throughout the history of the church and its leaders. In the histories of Israel, the church, and many nations a call to fasting has heightened the importance of a need, bringing the earnestness of circumstances to the attention of others and to the Lord.

The purpose of fasting must be considered from two perspectives. One is the benefit it brings to us personally in our relationship with God. But the other is the wider benefit it brings to the Kingdom of God. Sometimes the latter does not directly profit us. Fasting is often a way of paying the price in order that others might benefit.

The biblical message seems clear. Fasting, when undertaken righteously, is a spiritual discipline that God is pleased with and is effective in achieving goals that might otherwise be unobtainable. Although much of our focus in a fast is on what we deny ourselves, part of the significance from God's perspective is what is achieved in our own spiritual life. Here are some suggestions, based on my own experience. At the end of the book I have included more specific examples of how this has played out in my life.

Growing in Christ

This is the most fundamental purpose of fasting. When I began the fasting journey in my teens I sensed that such a commitment pleased the Lord as well as introduced me to Him. This deepening intimacy with Christ happened in a number of ways. I could spend time with the Lord for an hour or so each day because I was not eating. Having the extra time allowed me to pray—often just waiting on the Lord or learning to listen to Him, rather than doing lots of intercession.

Other things changed as well. I began to experience some pain in my fasting, and this challenged my will. I found not eating, and the breaking of the routines of eating, to be hard. My body, like anyone else's, rebelled. My will was firm; once I had decided not to eat that was the end of the matter. But having the will did not stop the hunger or the temptation, or the breaking of the eating cycle. I also began to learn that we cannot stop the Enemy from tempting us, but we can stop him from doing us damage.

An illustration of the purpose of fasting was that when I fasted from lunch while at Bible college, eating only fruit, I could then spend time praying with friends such as Steve. Our prayer times may not have had measurable goals like my later fasts did, but they increased my passion for what is now called the 10/40 Window. We were praying for Central

Asia to open up to the Gospel, for God to somehow allow us to move into those countries. We had no idea at the time that it would actually happen! But this discipline began to help us engage with just how much the Lord loved this part of the world.

These missed meals didn't cripple me physically. In fact, they helped keep me fit and healthy! I had no life-changing purpose in mind with this fasting, but it became one way for me to take part in the Great Commission, my calling in Christ to help build the Kingdom of God.

Another example of how this intimacy with Christ grew in me was that even between prayer times I could still sense a focus on the Lord. Though maybe not focusing specifically on Him, I began to realize He was still at my side.

Self-Denial

The essence of fasting is self-denial. Every fast, in some way, is a denial of our way of life. Every fast takes us into the death of self, its desires and often its physical needs. From God's perspective, this is a major benefit! Life becomes a little more God-centered and a little less self-centered.

In the act of surrender to the discipline of fasting we are voluntarily choosing to enter into a type of self-denial that can naturally invoke a brokenness of spirit if we let it. The Lord will not normally humble us, as this is something we should do for ourselves (James 4:10). We surrender to the humiliation of fasting to gain more of the presence and purposes of the Kingdom of God in our lives and in the lives of those for whom we may be fasting.

In the act of the denial of fasting we are choosing to submit to the "sackcloth and ashes," the shame and the weakness that fasting brings. It is embarrassing to discover that missing even one meal is a battle for us, or that we become bad-tempered when trying to fast for twelve hours.

As an extreme example, when I am doing an extended fast I don't have the strength in my arms to carry my large business briefcase, which also contains my laptop. So I am reduced to letting a colleague carry it, or taking just my pad and pencil to work or meetings.

But this process of self-denial goes further. The very act of fasting is itself a way of choosing to make ourselves more vulnerable. The routines and habits we rely upon are undone. When I fast, I am fragile. The discipline of fasting does not engender strength in me, but weakness. Though I have met people who told me that they feel stronger, this has not been my normal experience. Quite the opposite has proven true. I have to reschedule my life, removing all the demanding activities. Even taking out the garbage or carrying in the groceries from the car can be too much. It is humbling to have to admit that you cannot do the things you usually do, or that you aren't feeling too well.

The denial of self means that you have to accept that the normally arrogant, strong self is not in charge anymore, and that without it you feel quite weak and exposed. Though humiliating for this to happen, it can lead to a deeper humility and brokenness of spirit.

Your Will Takes Precedence over Your Body

The denial of the fast also impacts the way you are as a person. By denying yourself something you want and have relied upon, you are changing all your basic priorities. Things are turned upside down. You will look at your life from a different perspective, as those elements that have propped up your day-to-day existence are withdrawn. You encounter elements of yourself of which you may have been unaware.

When you are abstaining from food there is an added dimension. You are no longer living to eat, or eating to live. You are doing neither. Instead, you are saying to your body, *Shut up! Be quiet! Stop moaning!* It can moan quite a lot, even if you simply miss your usual evening meal.

Your fast is placing your spirit and will over and above your body's needs. You are entering a time of significant self-denial where you are exploring what will happen to you physically as you stop eating. You have not been here before with your body. This is a first.

But something much deeper is also happening. You are shifting your priorities so that you have time on your hands that would otherwise be used to meet your appetites. You are telling your body you are in control of the situation, and you are not going to allow your physical self to have its wishes. Such rights, demands, and appetites are at an end for a season. There are other things in life that you are placing at the top of your list, above your physical needs. So your body should be silent while you get on with the far more important task of self-denial.

Affirming Your Earnestness

As part of asserting your will over your body you are also making declarations about the seriousness of your intent. This is an act of sacrifice. The stakes are higher; the intensity of your commitment is stronger. The daily routine of your life is interrupted. Instead of competing with other demands, through your fast you can engage a depth of priority that you would not find any other way.

I often hear people say that they could never fast. They don't want to give up an aspect of their life for a season, especially if that aspect is food! But I know they could do it if they wanted to and were willing to begin to practice. The psychology is simple. We are always faithful to our own personal needs. We all have a basic instinct to put ourselves first, though few of us ever consciously admit this. We all have the tendency to deny that we can do something, if we don't want to do it, while often somewhat deviously affirming outwardly that we wish we could. What we don't admit to ourselves is that we will not do what we do not want to do. We all find the will to do what we want to do. By choosing to fast we are making a commitment to fully cooperate with ourselves in allowing this to happen.

My point is that we must be serious about the discipline of the process. We are choosing not to waiver, even though we have no idea what will happen. We are not going to change our minds when we get our first headache, or discover that we overlooked a dinner date—the perfect excuse to stop fasting. What I am commending here is the mindset of the hunger striker. We can learn much from such people. I am not necessarily commending the cause, just the dedication. Fasting is the ultimate eyes-ahead, regardless-of-the-cost, focused commitment, whether for one day, three days, or longer.

Or it is like the soldier, under orders from his commander, who walks into the oncoming fire bracing himself for the shells. He will not run, cower, or hide. Most men at one time or another feel this type of call on their lives. They just need to get on and do it. Women likewise can have the same mindset taking on the risk of childbirth. You are dead serious.

But such uncompromising resolve impacts us in other ways as well.

Surrender to Christ

Perhaps the most significant purpose of a fast for most of us will be the act of love in submission to Christ. If you are open to the idea of fasting to the Lord, He could easily lead you into a fast for no other reason than obedience or surrender to Him. Your reason for fasting could simply be nothing more than the fact that the Lord requires or invites you to do so. Our discipleship journey is one of increasing surrender to Christ as part of our growing Christ-likeness. Fasting is a very tangible way of achieving this.

Fasting as Prayer

Of course, whatever the specific reason for fasting, it is always an act of intercession. Its core benefit is to unleash more of God's purposes by standing in allegiance with Christ. Fasting for me, personally, has had very little to do with the Enemy, though that may be the case for some. Fasting has always been between Father God and me. Regardless of what I am fasting for—the nation or renewal, knowledge or money—the nature of the fasts and their function all tend to be quite different. One thing all of them have had in common, however, is that a prolonged fast is its own prayer: praying in an intercessory way as you are before God. Throughout a fast you need to see your life as prayer.

During a shorter water-only fast it is easy to see the fast as simply missing a meal. I would discourage you from this. Think of it as a four-hour fast, or as a six-, eight-, twelve-, or twenty-four-hour fast. When you start your fast, your act of intercession begins, even if the next mealtime is several hours away. Be aware that you are fasting, even if you are taking the children to school or functioning in your normal employment. You may spend the mealtime in prayer instead of eating, but that is simply a more concentrated part of the intercession that began several hours earlier.

Although I find it difficult to pray in the traditional posture of bended knee during extended fasts, the essence of the fast itself is intercessory prayer. Your life, pain, and obedience are the intercession. Here your weakened physical condition and its submission is your prayer. Your fasting is itself your plea to the Lord. The very act of fasting is a declaration to the Lord of what you desire. It is an act of importunity, your persistent hammering on the doors of heaven—but in a meek and humble way that is brought about by your devitalized condition. *Listen! Look at me! I am in earnest! I am desperate! I am in great need! Answer me, please!*

As the days go by during an extended fast, just staying on the fast is the major victory each day; and your life and condition are your prayers to the Lord. Just continuing in obedience is enough. After the initial period of settling into the fast, it can get easier for a few days—though you remain aware that what you are doing is prayer, that God is listening. But later I have regularly experienced a deep weariness, not caused by the lack of food but merely by the length of time. This is when the intercession of your life bites deep. Your pain and its weariness becomes your prayer. You begin to realize that going further will become an even greater battle. At this time, especially, my life truly becomes my intercessory prayer. I become my own sacrifice.

A Means of Change

Another common purpose and benefit of fasting is that it achieves change where it previously has not been possible. This change can be either a personal matter or something related to others. It could be for a congregation or even for a nation. This is the kind of fast that we do when we need to break the mold. We need to make a new start, to break a deadlock.

A parallel in Scripture is when David turned around at the walls of Jebus, or Jerusalem, and said, "Whoever leads the attack on the Jebusites will become commander-in-chief" (1 Chronicles 11:6). Joab was over the wall first, and lived on as commander of the army for almost all of David's reign. Someone had to break the deadlock and move forward. When Joab did so, then everyone else could follow.

Fasting is a spiritual weapon, like Joab himself was on this occasion. It is the act of the spiritual warrior, the leader, the commander, the captain. It is the men or women who take authority by taking responsibility for the need for change. They step out, and through their fast they begin to possess what change is needed. I have numerous personal examples of this, but the one I especially recall was when our business was close to marketing a key product and we didn't have enough money to launch it. The normal sources, like banks, were closed to us. The future of the company depended on it, so I fasted and began to see the necessary funds come in.

I have won most of the battles in which I have engaged. I believe my failure rate has been greatly reduced because I was merely following the Lord in these conflicts. Fasting is one of the ways we can "turn up the volume" in helping to win a battle. By this I mean that we can, through fasting, bring a much greater pressure for positive change to bear on spiritual reality.

Often I have found myself talking to the Lord about a fast for some time before I actually enter the fast. A fast normally grows on me over a month or two, because fasting is always the final act. Fasting is the final form of intercession, when everything else has failed. You may sense you have the answer already, but you know you need to act by taking authority and responsibility over the situation to actually change it. Your prayer will be your action. You are now taking authority, confident that the fast you are on will deliver what you need if you act in obedience and humility. All of my fasts have been based on very specific goals. These goals themselves become the prayer.

Repentance

Repentance as a nation or self-denial before battle in war is another kind of fast. Fasting preceded historic moments in Israel's history and the church's history. We can observe three such fasts in Scripture. In one we see the Law of God being given through Moses (Exodus 34:28), in other instances we see the Israelites fasting in times of crisis (Judges 20:24–26; 2 Chronicles 20:1–4), and then we see the perfecting of the Lamb of God. Jesus came out of the fasting temptations (Luke 4:1–13) in absolute purity, so by His life, which was His prayer, He could go to His death and bring about our life. Along similar lines, Daniel's fast recorded in Daniel 9 was prayer that brought about the salvation of Israel. By changing our focus away from our day-to-day life, God's perspective can become clearer, and such "truth" effectively enables our repentance (see 2 Timothy 2:25–26).

You may feel there is an area of your life or the life of another that you need to engage with a deeper repentance. Fasting is a significant way of focusing yourself on this goal.

Growth in Spiritual Gifting

I had always sensed that I had received a particular spiritual gift from the Lord at my conception. However, the ability to use this gift freely came only after I had done a specific fast. The obedience of the fast released it to me. Along similar lines I found myself fasting for money from the Lord that, in a sense, He had already provided through someone. He had told this person to give it to me. During the fast I realized that this man was waiting for me to ask, and only then would I see the provision I was seeking.

When our ministry is made more effective through fasting, there is significant benefit to the Kingdom of God.

Engaging the Enemy

Perhaps you have a personal problem, or a stalemate with a person you are seeking to help, and it won't shift. Or maybe your congregation or house group is facing an obstacle. You have tried everything else; fasting is all that remains. You then do what Christ has told you to do. You are now cast upon the Lord in a last-hope bid to see the matter resolved. If you are experienced in fasting, you might commit to an extended fast.

But be careful. You should never be so presumptuous as to address the Enemy directly or pretend you have some spell or power over the demonic just because you are fasting. Normally you will be weaker, not stronger, in body and spirit. So it is important that in any and every fast your focus is on Christ Himself. He is your Lord and you answer to Him alone. It is from Him that you are seeking knowledge and change. You are not seeking some special power over the Enemy. The answer to your prayers and your fasting are with Christ, Son of the Living God, second Person of the Social Trinity and the author of all life.

As a result of your fast you may gain the knowledge that you need to break the power of the darkness. Alternately, you may simply discover that God has intervened in an apparently unrelated way and the problem no longer exists. Whatever the outcome, the balance of power in the spiritual world will be different because of your fast, and God will have more room to act.

Sharing in Christ's Sufferings

The essence of the Atonement is the giving of Christ's life to all those who will accept His sacrifice. It is Christ's death for our life, an act of voluntary love on His part that we can now appropriate for ourselves. In the same way that we accept this sacrifice of Christ we also accept the discipline of fasting. We surrender to it, suffering for a season and thereby choosing to associate with Christ in His surrendered sacrifice. This is the kind of attitude Paul had in mind when he suggested that to share in His glory we must also be willing to share in His sufferings (Romans 8:17).

As with baptism, I believe that as we go under the "waters" of fasting so we can rise again later into the life Christ has promised us all. For a season we voluntarily place ourselves under the waters of darkness, so that by our denial we are able to seek the Lord in a way we would not be able to in the normal routines of our life. Just claiming back the time we normally spend eating can provide an extra two to three hours per day, making a critical difference in our prayer and intercession life. We are standing with Christ for a season in a more sacrificial way.

In Summary

Two simple goals under-gird fasting. Initially fasting should be an act of knowing God better and deepening our relationship with Him. But it will soon evolve so that the ongoing goal will be to see change and breakthrough in areas where they would not otherwise be possible. The act of fasting should take you from sacrifice to clarity. We may not necessarily start with these battles. Simply learning how to fast is battle enough for some of us. But in time, as we grow in this discipline, fasting will become a treasured means of achieving a God-given goal that has remained elusive.

Of course, fasting is in part a mystery. We should never treat it as a formula, a way to manipulate God to give us what we are seeking. It must always remain Christ-centered and fully in submission to His purposes and priorities. For some of us it will be a weapon we use frequently. For others it may be more occasional. But I feel Scripture is clear that fasting will yield significant fruit for all who are willing to enter into the sufferings of Christ in this way.

As I close this chapter I would suggest that you give some thought to this question: If you were to start fasting, what would be your purpose? Would it be to learn more about this spiritual discipline? Perhaps you know that God wants to stretch you in new areas of your relationship with Him and this is one way of doing it. If so, fasting will represent a major step forward in your Christian life. Or perhaps your purpose for fasting would focus on a particular need you are facing. I will address these more specific goals later, helping you learn how to identify them.

Whatever your purpose for fasting, you have a demanding and yet rewarding journey ahead of you.

THE BIBLICAL BACKGROUND OF FASTING

Although the Bible does not have a lot to say about fasting, what it does say helps set the stage for the modern practice of the discipline. In this chapter I will outline some of the basic teaching from Scripture, quoting the verses using the New International Version text.

I will comment on these verses where helpful or necessary. I would encourage you to read the passages in their full context in your Bible, inviting the Lord to speak to you through the passages. We have much to learn about how to encourage each other to fast.

Old Testament Passages

Almost all major religions practice fasting. The motives for fasting in paganism are for defense and protection. For instance, in many religions it is thought that, following an individual's death, it is not wise to eat when the dead person's spirit is still around, as revenging spirits infect the food. Fasting is recommended.[1] Though we normally think of fasting in the context of food, other forms of abstinence were practiced as well. For example, the Israelites, along with other ancient societies, abstained from sexual relations prior to a battle.

In broad terms, the Old Testament references represent fasting as a discipline for seeking guidance, for suffering vicariously, and for expressing grief, penitence, brokenness, or humility. Fasting held a significant place in Israel's religious life, being mandated by law and required of all citizens. Though not mentioned frequently, it was part of the basic fabric of religious life in Israel.

Christianity today can be quite passive, as we expect others to look after us spiritually. Here in Scripture we see examples of God's people actively participating in a sacrificial way to achieve God's purposes. This is at the heart of the discipline of fasting. In Hebrew, the most common word for fasting has the same root as "to humble" or "to afflict" one's self or soul.[2] Affliction of oneself is seen as correction: of changing (i.e., repentance), or birthing, or bringing about a desired goal. In Psalm 119:71 the psalmist says, "It was good for me to be afflicted so that I might learn your decrees."

Preparation for Service. Fasting is associated with religious ritual in preparing oneself for sacred service, where individuals focus on their spiritual and emotional preparation and state, thereby denying their physical needs. The following Scriptures echo this practice of afflicting oneself as a purification rite in the context of the Day of Atonement:

---

1   F. S. Rothenberg, "Fasting," in C. Brown, ed., *The New International Dictionary of New Testament Theology* (Exeter, UK: Paternoster, 1971), 611–14.

2   P. Wenger, "to humble" (semantic field 6700), in W. A. van Gemeren, ed., *The New International Dictionary of Old Testament Theology and Exegesis* (Carlisle, UK: Paternoster, 1996), 451.

This is to be a lasting ordinance for you: On the tenth day of the seventh month you must deny yourselves and not do any work—whether native-born or an alien living among you—because on this day atonement will be made for you, to cleanse you. (Leviticus 16:29–30)

The tenth day of this seventh month is the Day of Atonement. Hold a sacred assembly and deny yourselves, and present an offering made to the Lord by fire. (Leviticus 23:27)

A Facet of Prayer. Fasting can be both an essential attitude and practice for a person conversing with God.

When I went up on the mountain to receive the tablets of stone, the tablets of the covenant that the Lord had made with you, I stayed on the mountain forty days and forty nights; I ate no bread and drank no water. (Deuteronomy 9:9, See also Exodus 34:28.)

David pleaded with God for the child. He fasted and went into his house and spent the nights lying on the ground. The elders of his household stood beside him to get him up from the ground, but he refused, and he would not eat any food with them. (2 Samuel 12:16–17)

So we fasted and petitioned our God about this, and he answered our prayer. (Ezra 8:23)

When I heard these things, I sat down and wept. For some days I mourned and fasted and prayed before the God of heaven. (Nehemiah 1:4)

So I turned to the Lord God and pleaded with him in prayer and petition, in fasting, and in sackcloth and ashes. (Daniel 9:3)

It was following Moses' fast that he was given the Ten Commandments. This was a supernatural fast. Not eating for forty days is possible, but going without water for that period is practically impossible. Most people could go without water for only two or three days before doing serious damage to their body. Moses was clearly supernaturally sustained by God during his fast. When God wants to begin a new thing He always accompanies it with the supernatural, and fasting is often part of that process.

Times of Peril. The Israelites called for fasts when there was a danger of war or plague or at critical moments in their history.

When the Benjamites came out from Gibeah to oppose them, they cut down another eighteen thousand Israelites, all of them armed with swords. Then the Israelites, all the people, went up to Bethel, and there they sat weeping before the Lord. They fasted that day until evening and presented burnt offerings and fellowship offerings to the Lord. (Judges 20:25–26)

Uriah said to David, "The ark and Israel and Judah are staying in tents, and my master Joab and my lord's men are camped in the open fields. How could I go to my house to eat and drink and lie with my wife? As surely as you live, I will not do such a thing!" (2 Samuel 11:11)

Some men came and told Jehoshaphat, "A vast army is coming against you from Edom, from the other side of the Sea. It is already in Hazazon Tamar" (that is, En Gedi).

Alarmed, Jehoshaphat resolved to enquire of the Lord, and he proclaimed a fast for all Judah. (2 Chronicles 20:2–3)

Dispatches were sent by couriers to all the king's provinces with the order to destroy, kill and annihilate all the Jews— young and old, women and little children—on a single day, the thirteenth day of the twelfth month, the month of Adar, and to plunder their goods. A copy of the text of the edict was to be issued as law in every province and made known to the people of every nationality so they would be ready for that day. . . . In every province to which the edict and order of the king came, there was great mourning among the Jews, with fasting, weeping and wailing. (Esther 3:13–14; 4:3)

Then Esther sent this reply to Mordecai: "Go, gather together all the Jews who are in Susa, and fast for me. Do not eat or drink for three days, night or day. I and my maids will fast as you do. When this is done, I will go to the king, even though it is against the law. And if I perish, I perish." (Esther 4:15–16)

What the locust swarm has left the great locusts have eaten; what the great locusts have left the young locusts have eaten; what the young locusts have left other locusts have eaten. . . . Declare a holy fast; call a sacred assembly. Summon the elders and all who live in the land to the house of the Lord your God, and cry out to the Lord. (Joel 1:4,14)

Fasting was also used to call out to God for a safe journey:

There, by the Ahava Canal, I proclaimed a fast, so that we might humble ourselves before our God and ask him for a

safe journey for us and our children, with all our posses-
sions. (Ezra 8:21)

Breaking Oppression. It was practiced when a person or the nation
was oppressed by great problems. Sometimes accompanied by the mocking of others:

> "David pleaded with God for the child. He fasted and went
> into his house and spent the nights lying on the ground. The
> elders of his household stood beside him to get him up from
> the ground. But he refused, and he would not eat any food
> with them." (2 Samuel 12:16–23)

> "Yet when they were ill, I put on sackcloth and humbled
> myself with fasting. When my prayers returned to me un-
> answered, I went about mourning as though for my friend
> or brother . . . But when I stumbled, they gathered in glee;
> attackers gathered against me when I was unaware, they
> slandered me without ceasing." (Psalm 35:13–15)

> "When I weep and fast, I must endure scorn." (Psalm 69:10)

Confession and Cleansing. Fasting is associated with repentance.
Crying out to God for spiritual cleansing can be accompanied by fasting.

> Samuel said, "Assemble all Israel at Mizpah and I will inter-
> cede with the Lord for you." When they had assembled at
> Mizpah, they drew water and poured it out before the Lord.
> On that day they fasted and there they confessed, "We have
> sinned against the Lord." (1 Samuel 7:5–6)

When Ahab heard these words, he tore his clothes, put on sackcloth and fasted. He lay in sackcloth and went around meekly. (1 Kings 21:27)

On the twenty-fourth day of the same month, the Israelites gathered together, fasting and wearing sackcloth and having dust on their heads. . . . They stood in their places and confessed their sins and the wickedness of their fathers. (Nehemiah 9:1–2)

Jonah started into the city. He proclaimed: "Forty more days and Nineveh will be overturned." The Ninevites believed God. They declared a fast, and all of them, from the greatest to the least, put on sackcloth. (Jonah 3:4–5)

This type of fasting was ordained in the Law of Moses for the Day of Atonement:

The Lord said to Moses, "The tenth day of this seventh month is the Day of Atonement. Hold a sacred assembly and deny yourselves, and present an offering made to the Lord by fire. Do no work on that day, because it is the Day of Atonement, when atonement is made for you before the Lord your God. Anyone who does not deny himself on that day must be cut off from his people. . . . It is a sabbath of rest for you, and you must deny yourselves. From the evening of the ninth day of the month until the following evening you are to observe your sabbath." (Leviticus 23:26–32)

An Act of Remembrance. Following the destruction of Jerusalem in 586 BC, four fast days were instituted as a way of remembering four specific events associated with those lamentable days.

> Then the word of the Lord Almighty came to me: "Ask all
> the people of the land and the priests, 'When you fasted and
> mourned in the fifth and seventh months for the past sev-
> enty years, was it really for me that you fasted?'" (Zechariah
> 7:4–5)

> Again the word of the Lord Almighty came to me. This is
> what the Lord Almighty says: "The fasts of the fourth, fifth,
> seventh and tenth months will become joyful and glad occa-
> sions and happy festivals for Judah. Therefore love truth and
> peace." (Zechariah 8:18–19)

In Times of Loss. Fasting is frequently associated with times of
mourning.

> Then David and all the men with him took hold of their
> clothes and tore them. They mourned and wept and fasted
> till evening for Saul and his son Jonathan, and for the army
> of the Lord and the house of Israel, because they had fallen
> by the sword. (2 Samuel 1:11–12)

Fasting also exposed personal inner torment:

> I am poor and needy, and my heart is wounded within me.
> . . . My knees give way from fasting; my body is thin and
> gaunt. (Psalm 109:22, 24)

National or Regional Fasts. Calling a fast of the whole nation was
not uncommon during a crisis. Many of the Scriptures I have cited were
fasts called by the leaders of the nation or a region or town. As a modern
example of something similar, during the darkest days of World War II
Britain was called to fast and pray in light of the imminent threat of

invasion from Hitler's Germany. The invasion never came, and instead the Allies were able to invade Europe and bring the war to an end.

Length. Though the lengths of fasts varied, they often lasted from morning until evening:

> Then the Israelites, all the people, went up to Bethel, and there they sat weeping before the Lord. They fasted that day until evening and presented burnt offerings and fellowship offerings to the Lord. (Judges 20:26)

As we have seen, David and his men fasted till evening upon hearing of the deaths of Saul and Jonathan (2 Samuel 1:11–12), and the fast accompanying the Day of Atonement lasted from the evening of one day till the evening of the next day (Leviticus 23:32). After Saul's death some of the Israelites fasted for seven days (1 Samuel 31:13).

Ineffective Fasting. Not every fast recorded in the Old Testament was pleasing to the Lord. God took exception to the hypocrisy of Israel's fasts, and the prophets declared that without right conduct fasting was in vain.

> "Why have we fasted," they say, "and you have not seen it? Why have we humbled ourselves, and you have not noticed?" Yet on the day of your fasting, you do as you please and exploit all your workers. Your fasting ends in quarreling and strife, and in striking each other with wicked fists. You cannot fast as you do today and expect your voice to be heard on high. Is this the kind of fast I have chosen, only a day for a man to humble himself? Is it only for bowing one's head like a reed and for lying on sackcloth and ashes? Is that what you call a fast, a day acceptable to the Lord?

Is not this the kind of fasting I have chosen: to loose the chains of injustice and untie the cords of the yoke, to set the oppressed free and break every yoke? Is it not to share your food with the hungry and to provide the poor wanderer with shelter—when you see the naked, to clothe him, and not to turn away from your own flesh and blood? (Isaiah 58:3–7)

Then the Lord said to me, "Do not pray for the well-being of this people. Although they fast, I will not listen to their cry; though they offer burnt offerings and grain offerings, I will not accept them. Instead, I will destroy them with the sword, famine and plague." (Jeremiah 14:11–12)

Ask all the people of the land and the priests, "When you fasted and mourned in the fifth and seventh months for the past seventy years, was it really for me that you fasted?" (Zechariah 7:4–5)

Though it is evident that not every fast is a success, that should not stop us from practicing the discipline. But we must always be cautious about measuring fasting by outcomes. Some of my longest fasts had the least visible positive outcomes at the time. I have entered fasts in which afterward I could see they were only for the purpose of breaking my eating habit or my presumption about food or money. We should always ask ourselves, *What has the fast done within me? How have I been changed by the fast?*

New Testament Passages

Considering the significance of fasting in the Old Testament period, there are relatively few references to the practice in the Synoptics (the first three Gospels) and very little elsewhere in the New Testament. However, historian Oskar Skarsaune demonstrates that fasting, like other aspects of Jewish religious life, found its way into the early church.[3] Since fasting was such a well-established part of Jewish religious tradition, it is safe to assume that as Jesus grew up He would have been drilled in its practice. Prior to his public ministry, I feel quite certain that Jesus regularly practiced fasting during the religious fasts of Judaism.

By the time of Christ there were two established fast days per week. In Jesus' parable of the Pharisee and the tax collector, the Pharisee congratulated himself for fasting twice a week (Luke 18:12). Fasting, however, was not a practice needed by Christ's disciples during His earthly ministry:

> Now John's disciples and the Pharisees were fasting. Some people came and asked Jesus, "How is it that John's disciples and the disciples of the Pharisees are fasting, but yours are not?"
> Jesus answered, "How can the guests of the bridegroom fast while he is with them? They cannot, so long as they have him with them. But the time will come when the bridegroom will be taken from them, and on that day they will fast." (Mark 2:18–20)

This has led some to argue that because we now have Christ and we are in a new period of history with God, fasting is no longer required. This argument can be supported in part by the very sparse evidence in the New Testament of the practice among believers. But in reality the argument that the practice has been superseded by Jesus Himself is not valid for several reasons. Scripture hints at the possibility that Christ may have merely suspended fasting among His immediate disciples for

---

1   Oskar Skarsaune, *In the Shadow of the Temple: Jewish Influences on Early Christianity* (Downers Grove, IL: InterVarsity, 2002), 363.

the three years He was training them, while assuming that following His departure His disciples would fast:

> Jesus answered, "Can you make the guests of the bridegroom fast while he is with them? But the time will come when the bridegroom will be taken from them; in those days they will fast." (Luke 5:34–39)

Jesus instructed His followers how to fast properly, avoiding drawing attention to themselves. Clearly His intention was to ensure that a new code of conduct would accompany fasting in the lives of His followers. Traditions and practices needed to change when His followers fasted:

> When you fast, do not look somber as the hypocrites do, for they disfigure their faces to show men they are fasting. I tell you the truth, they have received their reward in full. But when you fast, put oil on your head and wash your face, so that it will not be obvious to men that you are fasting, but only to your Father, who is unseen; and your Father, who sees what is done in secret, will reward you. (Mathew 6:16–18)

In Matthew 17 we read about Jesus healing and delivering a boy who suffered from seizures as a result of a demon. When Jesus' disciples asked Him why they had been unable to drive out the demon, He answered, "Because you have so little faith" (Matthew 17:20). Jesus then assured them, "Nothing will be impossible for you." Though its textual credibility has been questioned by scholars involved in newer Bible translations, the footnote of the New International Version records that Jesus also said: "But this kind does not go out except by prayer and fasting" (Matthew 17:21). This is what the Lord has spoken about with me many times as part of my fasts.

I would contend, therefore, that Jesus taught that certain demonic enslavement necessitated fasting for healing, though we have no record of Him fasting in order to do this Himself. Nevertheless, He seems to be instructing us in finding keys to help people who are enslaved. In my own ministry experiences this teaching has proven true, as I will be illustrating later.

As noted earlier, Oskar Skarsaune makes a compelling case that the early church naturally adopted a number of Jewish ritual practices, from the Seder (sacred meal), to meeting for hymns and exaltation, to the writing of literature to maintain the traditions and values taught by Christus.[4] I believe it is also safe to assume that the first believers adopted practices regarding the importance of fasting, as seen in the following verses:

> While they were worshiping the Lord and fasting, the Holy Spirit said, "Set apart for me Barnabas and Saul for the work to which I have called them." So after they had fasted and prayed, they placed their hands on them and sent them off. (Acts 13:2–3)

> Paul and Barnabas appointed elders for them in each church and, with prayer and fasting, committed them to the Lord, in whom they had put their trust. (Acts 14:23)

Three times in his letters Paul referred to his fasting, though the fasting might not have always been voluntary!

---

2   Much of Skarsaune's book, *In the Shadow of the Temple*, pertains to this topic.

I have labored and toiled and have often gone without sleep; I have known hunger and thirst and have often gone without food; I have been cold and naked. (2 Corinthians 11:27, See also 1 Corinthians 4:11 and 2 Corinthians 6:5.)

Jesus fasted for forty days prior to the commencement of His ministry. This was a unique moment in Christ's life, as we do not read that He fasted again. Only Moses and Elijah shared the experience of a forty-day fast.

Jesus was led by the Spirit into the desert to be tempted by the devil. After fasting forty days and forty nights, he was hungry. (Matthew 4:1–2)

Moses was there with the Lord forty days and forty nights without eating bread or drinking water. And he wrote on the tablets the words of the covenant—the Ten Commandments. (Exodus 34:28)

Elijah was afraid and ran for his life. When he came to Beersheba in Judah, he left his servant there, while he himself went a day's journey into the desert. He came to a broom tree, sat down under it and prayed that he might die. . . . Then he lay down under the tree and fell asleep.
All at once an angel touched him and said, "Get up and eat." He looked around, and there by his head was a cake of bread baked over hot coals, and a jar of water. He ate and drank and then lay down again.
The angel of the Lord came back a second time and touched him and said, "Get up and eat, for the journey is too much for you." So he got up and ate and drank. Strengthened by

that food, he traveled forty days and forty nights until he reached Horeb, the mountain of God. (1 Kings 19:3–8)

These three fasts symbolize three significant stages related to the birth of the church. Moses was the Lawgiver, Elijah was the Prophet applying the Law, and Jesus was the King fulfilling the Law. Each stage was accompanied by a forty-day fast.

Though Scripture does not hint that we need to take up the practice of a forty-day fast, I find clear biblical evidence that through fasting we can participate in seeing breakthroughs in specific areas of our own lives and the lives of others, as well as in our churches, towns, and other areas. I would conclude, therefore, that fasting is a spiritual discipline that God encourages us to develop and to learn to use effectively.

Adopted by the Church?

What we see in the Old Testament is a kind of recidivism, or backsliding: the people of Israel embracing covenant relationship with the Lord but then compromising their commitment through sins of greed, selfishness, and unwillingness to follow the Law of Moses. Fasting followed this pattern and expressed the same ebb and flow, being undermined by human baggage and sin. Nevertheless, the practice of fasting continued to be part of the religious life of Israel into the postexilic period—surviving even to the time of Christ.

In the Synoptic Gospels we read that Jesus criticized the hypocritical practice of fasting. Christ himself fasted, however, as part of His preparation for ministry. And the early church doesn't seem to have questioned the value of the discipline.

In fact, fasting became a regular part of the spiritual disciplines of the church after the New Testament period, used as a valuable tool for self-humbling, intercession in crisis, and as a source of income for the poor—as believers gave to the needy either the food that they abstained from eating or the money they would have spent to buy food. What we see, some would say, is an overzealous commitment to fasting as a way of life. Fasting was practiced for a number of reasons, including breaking physical lust, disciplining the body, and progressing toward Christ-likeness and spiritual maturity.[5] Some of these values and principles are of importance to us now, as we shall note in due course.

Richard Foster, in his popular book, *Celebration of Discipline*, offers us a significant overview of the biblical and historical precedent of fasting: "The list of biblical personages who fasted becomes a 'Who's Who' of Scripture: Moses the lawgiver, David the king, Elijah the Prophet, Esther the queen, Daniel the seer, Anna the prophetess, Paul the apostle, Jesus Christ the incarnate Son. Many of the great Christians throughout church history fasted and witnessed to its value; among them were Martin Luther, John Calvin, John Knox, John Wesley, Jonathan Edwards, David Brainerd, Charles Finney and Pastor Hsi of China."[6]

---

3   Teresa Shaw has carefully reviewed this area in *The Burden of the Flesh: Fasting and Sexuality in Early Christianity* (Minneapolis: Fortress Press, 1998). Together with others, she has documented the move toward extreme behavior in suppressing physical needs, etc. The graphic detail of some of this behavior would be offensive to us today—especially women starving their bodies in order to look more masculine, following the Greek adoration of the male body (pp. 220–252). For those interested in more of the background of the post-New Testament church's attitudes toward fasting, see the appendix at the end of this book.

4   Richard Foster, *Celebration of Discipline: The Path to Spiritual Growth* (New York: Harper and Row), 42.

4.

AREAS OF ABSTINENCE

In this chapter we are going to look in a broad way at the concept of fasting. Over the years, most of my fasts have meant denying myself food. But on numerous occasions the Lord has touched other areas of my life I have needed to surrender to Him. You too may want or need to look at a fast that is not food-related. These can be effective spiritually, while sometimes being less demanding on your physical and emotional health. This may be where you need to begin in learning how to fast.

All fasting, by its very nature, targets that which is important to us, that which we value highly. This principle is at the heart of fasting: a denial of what we want, what we feel we need, or what we are using to help us cope with daily life. It is only when we consider fasting that we begin to discover those things we depend upon—our "soft addictions."

The types of fast one can do are endless. Most books on fasting will mention a variety of fasts that could be relevant to the reader.

The Concept of Abstinence

Behind all of our behavior we are making choices: choices to do this, not to do that, take this, change that, and so on. In fasting we choose to *abstain* from something—to refuse to do something that we normally do. Fasting is about denying ourselves something that we routinely enjoy.

When we ask ourselves what kind of fast we are going to do, the issue is what we are going to *abstain from*. Some would argue that fasting is a time of *doing something,* such as praying. But we will normally be able to do this one thing only if we have abstained from other things.

So what will you abstain from in your fasting? The answers are endless, because the level of abstinence and the kind of thing(s) we abstain from depend on how big a statement we want to make to the Lord and the Enemy. For instance, not watching TV for a week is not nearly as much abstinence as giving your TV away!

In answering this question, therefore, you must set your own rules. But the key rule in this decision-making process is that *you must begin small*. Don't try to run before you can walk. You do not need to start your journey of fasting by denying yourself the thing you love most in the world. Abstaining from coffee, for example, may be a good idea but if you are addicted to coffee, it might be too demanding a place to start.

In deciding on the type of fast, you must take into account your lifestyle and the people around you. Fasting from food is feasible if you sit at a desk all day. But if you are a construction worker you will probably have to try abstaining from something other than food. Otherwise you may not be able to carry your load—literally! And being a grouch is not helpful to those close to you.

Therefore, a first step could be to list on a sheet of paper the things that come to mind that you could abstain from as a form of fasting. I would be surprised if you couldn't think of at least twenty things.

Fasting for me has fallen into two distinct areas. Fasting from food is the one type of fast, and fasting from other things is the other. Some people carry such hate for their bodies that they can starve themselves for a week and not notice. For others missing just a mere snack causes panic, as their stomachs growl in pain and discontent. So your first decision is what path of abstinence you are going down: food or non-food.

Fasting from Things Other Than Food

The idea of denial is much wider than abstaining from food or fluids. For instance, we might deny ourselves the use of our car for a week—or use it just for work and walk everywhere else. Alternately, we could keep the bicycle in the rack of the car and use it more. For some this would represent significant denial.

However, in our Western world one denial stands head and shoulders over most others: television. Turning off the TV would be one of our greatest sacrifices. Turning it off for a week—spending the time instead reading Scripture, visiting friends, or enjoying meeting the Lord in a good Christian book—would be real denial.

I would put watching TV in the same category as addictions to food and other compulsions. To stop watching TV shows and/or new or rented DVDs would be a sacrifice indeed for most of us. Many of us live in denial of what is really important to us or what we are addicted to, especially TV. We are in total control of what is likely the ultimate pacifier, and therefore many of us waste several hours a day watching TV. Abstaining from TV for, say, a week could be a valid fast, providing we choose a productive alternative to fill the time. (No, not playing video or computer games!) Many folks would be lost without the comforter called TV. Would you?

Many other soft addictions are possible targets for fasting abstinence. An article I read recently suggested that we all have about five hundred addictions and compulsions from which to choose. Anything we are capable of enjoying to excess can become an addiction for us. So denial via fasting can be a good idea.

What are your potential soft addictions? Some are edible, like coffee, chocolate, and other snacks. Others are far subtler. One of the most common is spending money we do not have by using credit cards or other forms of debt. For some of us, curbing our lifestyle and eliminating our debts would be an act of profound sacrifice. I'm not talking about a home mortgage, but other voluntary debts that we can easily accumulate.

Another form of denial that would be a real sacrifice for some would be to put a pornography block or filter on their computer. For others it could be smoking or chewing tobacco, drinking alcohol, eating out repeatedly, or buying expensive clothes. A soft addiction for many is "soft" drinks!

When we are thinking about fasting we should never forget the host of things we enjoy that would result in genuine denial if we were to stop them for a season, in honor of the Lord. Many of these involve sins or baggage that we need to clear from our lives. Denial is the path to greater holiness in these areas.

I am hesitant to even mention one final area of denial. In this age of chronic sleep deprivation, most of us don't get enough sleep. Since the invention of electricity (and then TV and movies at home), most of us stay up too late and sleep neither long enough nor deeply enough. We are also guilty of waking before we complete our sleep cycles. The impact of this on our immune system and other body cycles is a serious problem today in the Western world.

But having said that, denial of sleep could be the basis of several types of fasts. Going without sleep for a night of prayer and meditation can be a genuine fast. The problem with losing more than a night's sleep is that your body begins to go into a form of shock similar to jet lag. For a couple of days after losing even one night's sleep most of us are incapable of making any serious or intelligent decisions. Look at your calendar and workload, then plan to do half a night, or perhaps even a whole night of prayer with friends, rather than sleep. This type of fasting is more common in some parts of Europe, or in countries where Christianity is illegal, than it is at present in USA.

Alternately, you might choose to get up an hour earlier, for a period of time, as a fast. You could use this time to spend with the Lord in prayer and Bible study. You also could combine this with another fast, such as denying yourself tea or coffee until after your hour of prayer or doing a four-hour water-only fast.

Before moving on to look at abstaining from food and liquids it is important to mention one relevant principle. We should never deny ourselves things that would do us harm by abstaining from them. I am thinking of things like not taking our prescribed medicine, not wearing a motorcycle or bicycle helmet, or not seeing the doctor when we are sick. Instead of seeing such behavior as irrational, we can be tempted to argue that since we are doing it for the Lord He will protect and keep us. In reality, such behavior could be an offense against God and an irresponsible witness to others.

Denying Ourselves Food or Liquids

The critical rule regarding all fasting, but especially abstaining from food or liquids, is to start modestly. Let yourself grow gradually in the experience of denial, both in the type of fast and the length. I suggest that you begin cautiously, never underestimating the impact of either the act of denial on your body and spirit or your ability to absorb the sudden change.

With this in mind, let's look at some specific types of food and liquid fasts. As we go through these examples I will share some principles, based on my own experience, about learning to fast. You will see that sometimes there is a fine line between what is a fast and what is simply a healthy, responsible way of eating—adjustments that we may need to make for the rest of our lives. Although a fast is a time of specific denial, you may find that beginning a journey of fasting will also involve beginning a healthier overall relationship with your body.

My first and most important comment is that you must be careful not to deny yourself fluids. It is better to begin by not eating. For instance, miss one meal or deny yourself a favorite compulsive food like coffee or chocolate. Try several fasts like this, and then you will be ready to miss two meals. Let this build into more over time. As you gain experience, try a twenty-four-hour fast in which you deny all food, but drink plenty of liquids (more on that later). Each of these can be described as different types of fasts.

A One-Food-Only Fast

In this type of fast you eat one kind of food exclusively (along with drinking water). For a short period of time you can choose almost any kind of food, but choosing well can also be a health gain. For medical reasons, some people fast by eating just one fruit. Common choices are grapes, apples, a variety of juices, or even certain types of vegetables. These fasts suit most people and can be the easiest of all fasts.

I have done a number of these fasts. My favorite has been eating just grapes, plus drinking water. This can be particularly good in the autumn when grapes are plentiful and inexpensive. Some nutritionists will tell you that the best juice fasts are apple or grape. Grapes, especially black grapes, are one of the most holistic fruits. They have a great deal of fructose (natural sugar) and are almost all liquid. Because of their juicy flavor, for some this could be more of a delight than a fast! Other foods, such as apples, rice, or boiled potatoes, might be more appropriate.

Excluding One Food

Often called a partial fast, this is the opposite of the one-food-only fast. Here you are denying yourself just one item. But what item? Go for the most difficult to deny yourself, which for most of us is either coffee or chocolate. Tea (with lots of sugar?) likely comes a close second or third, probably followed by snack foods such as chips, cookies, and ice cream.

The time length of such fasts is something you will need to decide. On health grounds alone, some of us should fast from them for the rest of our lives! But we live in a culture addicted to caffeine, sugar, unhealthy snacks, and fast foods. If you don't want to drink beverages loaded with caffeine and/or sugar, for instance, then the only other options, other than water, may be juices and caffeine-free diet soft drinks. Many of these diet drinks, however, are high in aspartame, which some say is worse than sugar!

I most always resort to filtered, chilled water from our refrigerator water dispenser. Although I develop a strong dislike for water on my extended fasts, I do regain a taste for water afterwards. Having said that, we have few alternatives to water or natural juices if we do not want to return to addictive and unhealthy beverages. So, like others, I have compromised, drinking mostly water and diet drinks, along with no more than one cup of coffee a day.

A Water-Only Fast

This is the type of fast I practice most often. A water-only fast has numerous merits in addition to its spiritual benefits. Such a fast will be a health gain for you if you are physically capable of doing it. The health benefits include discovering what might be wrong with you, especially in regard to your stomach, kidneys, and digestive tract, and letting your stomach and digestive system rest for a while. During an extended fast, however, such benefits wane as the grueling days of the fast slowly move on.

One of the long-term physical benefits of water-only fasting is that with an ongoing healthy diet (see my discussion of the "Daniel fast" later) you will not regain the weight that you lose. In fact, you will even continue to lose weight if you exercise and eat moderate-sized portions.

I must warn you that my years of fasting left me with an aversion to water in almost any form, a problem that has taken me years to overcome. When doing a water-only fast I sometimes add a little lemon juice to reduce the water's bitterness. The important thing is that there is no nourishment in the water, which allows you to know that you are denying your body of any benefit beyond the water.

On the other hand, a variation of the water-only fast is to drink a liquid other than water. But be careful about drinking diet beverages. Some health scientists are warning us about artificial sweeteners like aspartame and saccharin. Taken over long periods of time they apparently can be dangerous.[1] What is becoming obvious is that almost anything in excess is harmful.

An Absolute Fast

This is when you neither eat nor drink. Nothing at all passes your lips. Although I have done this on rare occasion for up to a day, I have met people who have done absolute fasts for up to three days. I don't recommend this type of fast, and would go further and strongly caution against it. Moses fasted on Mount Sinai for forty days without eating or drinking (Exodus 34:28), but this was supernatural. It probably won't be when you do it! The other fasts mentioned in Scripture that were clearly "absolute" all arose from dire emergencies (see Esther 4:6–16; Jonah 3:4–9; Acts 9:3–9).

---

1 Janet Starr Hull, *Sweet Poison: How the World's Most Popular Artificial Sweetener Is Killing Us—My Story* (New York: New Horizon Press, 2000).

It is normally impossible for the human body to sustain an absolute fast for any length of time. The real danger is in the denial of liquids to the body. People have been known to live for ten to fourteen days without water. But doing so is highly discouraged. For someone with fragile health such a fast could kick in a range of problems, such as damage to the kidneys and a weakening of the immune system. So although the absolute fast is an act of unusually deep penitence, it should only be practiced in the most severe of circumstances and under clear direction from the Lord.

If you are led to do an absolute fast, do it for just a few hours. You will probably be shocked at how difficult it is. Side effects like the drying of the mouth are unpleasant and unavoidable. Rinsing out your mouth is not permitted in my opinion. Friends have told me that during this fast they have unthinkingly wandered over to the tap and filled a glass. Doing such a fast for twenty-four hours can be debilitating. During the second day some people feel they are going mad without liquids. You begin to wonder, *Should I moisten my lips, or is that cheating?*

My recommendation in regard to an absolute fast is, simply, *Don't go there!* I see little merit, and many more hazards, in comparison to a water-only fast.

In Summary

For some, choosing what to abstain from will be an easy decision. If you are a chef, tasting food is an essential part of your professional life. On days that you are working, you will need to find alternatives that are far more practical. But if you work behind a desk all day, then abstinence from food might be a way forward.

You may be overweight, in which case fasting from food may also be of benefit in breaking unhealthy eating habits. If you have to admit that you spend many hours a week in front of a TV, or some other addictive electronic device, then chances are you have discovered an activity from which to "fast."

The issue is how high you are willing to "turn up the volume." Where is your starting point? What would be both practical and sacrificial? You may find yourself giving more emphasis to either direction. Talk to others about your fasting choices, especially in regard to how they might be impacted.

Perhaps the most intimate, and important, question you need to answer is this: What do you *least* want to abstain from? Is that the place where you need to start?

In whatever area you begin, please start small—recognizing that even a minor abstinence will probably be a battle.

5.

VARIOUS TYPES OF FASTS

Deciding what to abstain from is one of the choices you must make when preparing to fast. The other is about the type of fast you will undertake. Will you be fasting privately or with a group? For how long will you fast? Most of my fasts are private, extended water-only fasts. This is the most demanding type of fast and is therefore likely to be the most effective. However, it will take most people quite some time to work up to this; and many will never take on this type of fast. In this chapter we will look at the various types of fasts you can undertake.

Occasional Short Fasts

This is where most people start. Whether denying yourself food or some other pleasure, an occasional fast that lasts six, twelve, or twenty-four hours is the most manageable. Nevertheless, you must treat it with the same sincerity as a longer fast. It is not insignificant just because it is short. But it does allow you to move gently into the discipline and to let the Lord instruct you. You are not necessarily making a commitment to do this type of fast again, as it is a one-time fast for a specific purpose.

Once you have decided what you are abstaining from you will be able to plan accordingly. If you are fasting from chocolate, then plan ahead so there is no chocolate in the house. Giving it away may be sacrifice enough! If you are abstaining from TV, then pull the plug out of the wall and put a cloth over the screen. You must get serious, even if only for a brief, occasional fast.

If you are doing a short water-only fast, don't presume that it will be easy. Some people are shocked when they first abstain from food. Your blood sugar level may drop and your instinct will be to rush for a chocolate bar. But then you will remember that you are supposed to be fasting, though I have known people who have impulsively eaten before realizing what they were doing. Such an outcome can be discouraging; but do not despair; things will change once you get into the rhythm of fasting. Another temptation is to binge during the meal before or after a fast. Both are equally unacceptable!

Intermittent Fasts

This is normally a regular act of abstinence, for example one day a week. You may abstain from food, or make some other sacrifice. This type of fast is a way of integrating the spiritual discipline of fasting into your life on an ongoing basis.

Some people might contend they are on an intermittent fast, perhaps abstaining one day a week from high-caffeine drinks, while knowing that in fact they really need to stop drinking so many of these beverages every day. Where is the pain or gain in abstaining for just one day a week? Others exercise instead of eating lunch, but thoroughly enjoy it. So where is the abstinence?

If a person is addicted to buying romance novels or music CDs, then to "fast" for one week every month might be a real jolt. Likewise, if you max out a bunch of credit cards on designer clothing, then you need to stop what you're doing—not just "fast." Be wise in your choice of what to abstain from, and be honest. An intermittent fast will be just as sacrificial as any other type, if you have chosen wisely.

I used to fast one meal every day: I would eat a good breakfast, then eat only fruit for lunch, then eat again in the evening. I did this for several years while in college. Another option is to follow the Catholic tradition of eating a reduced diet one day a week as a way of fasting. Some churches have a regular monthly day of prayer and fasting.

Partial fasts (denying yourself one or more specific foods) are useful because they help you establish a routine. Those close to you accept it as well. Such intermittent partial fasts are also the type of fast you might commit to if, as a group, you were undertaking a round-the-clock fast. Each of you commit to fast for a specific period on a rotating basis, so that there is always one person fasting. We have done this a number of times in our church, ministry, and business, often describing it as a "24/7 fast."

Longer Fasts

Longer fasts likewise can take the form of abstinence from food or some other sacrifice. Some good options for a non-food fast would be abstaining from watching TV from Monday to Friday, reading a biography of a great man or woman of God each week, or dedicating every evening for a week to praying with friends. Other things may need to get cancelled in order for you to do this.

A longer water-only fast might last from one to three days. If you are fasting from something other than food, your longer fast might last a week. Some use Lent as a time for a longer fast. Going through caffeine withdrawal by not drinking coffee or tea or eating chocolate could be a good Lenten fast. Or you could spend every evening reading Scripture rather than watching TV or DVDs. Abstaining from driving your car by traveling to work with someone else might be an appropriate sacrifice.

What is most significant about such fasts is their potential to change your lifestyle. A friend of mine encountered a huge battle when he committed to getting up half an hour earlier each day to spend time in prayer. He quickly found all kinds of reasons why he couldn't do it, until we sat down and began unpacking the obstacles. A year later he was still enjoying this time with the Lord, having moved on from the abstinence stage.

Extended Fasts

This is the hard path of fasting—choosing to give up something that you need or value for an extended period of time. One non-food extended fast would be to get up an hour earlier each day for a month in order to pray, worship, or read Scripture or a Christian book. Such a move can revolutionize our lives. To do this, we should also go to bed earlier.

In referring to "extended fasts" I am deliberately being vague. It isn't possible or even helpful to suggest a time period for an extended fast. The length of time will vary from one person to the next and will probably also increase as your experience of fasting grows. I would not recommend that you begin fasting with extended fasts.

Water-only extended fasts must be approached with particular care. This is discussed extensively later in the book, so I won't go into detail here.

Open-ended Fasts

Some extended fasts are open-ended, for example, where you make a commitment not to break your fast until your goals have been achieved.

Defining your goals is particularly important here. Again, this type of fast should not be considered until you have gained some experience. You must be particularly cautious if you are doing a water-only, open-ended fast.

Non-food fasts are also a possibility with this kind of fasting. One person I know woke early to study Hebrew for an hour each weekday, while another stopped at a parking lot on his way to work to spend time with the Lord. But in terms of their effects on a person, these types of open-ended fasts can't be compared to the open-ended water-only fast. *Don't even think about this kind of fast* until you have a proven track record and know what you are committing to.

Occasional Group Fasts

Most of my extended fasts have been private. But I have also participated in many group fasts. Such fasts can be called by a church or a group of churches or, on a larger scale, even to a nation during a time of crisis. Alternately, such fasts can be called by a small group or even by a Christian business. With the right leadership, calling groups to prayer and fasting can be a very powerful tool.

I must confess that I have a problem with some group fasts in that you fast, then you break the fast, then you get on with your life, and then you are frequently unable to measure whether you achieved anything. Group fasts can be a helpful way of introducing the discipline of fasting, but perhaps they could be better constructed so that one is able to measure the benefits. For instance, the group might agree on a sum of money that is needed and declare that openly as the goal. Or they might seek a person's healing, being specific about what they are asking of the Lord. This will help encourage more fasting. There will always be some benefits, even if it is merely that the faith community did something together. Set clear goals and live by them (see also the discussion of goals in chapter eight).

There are times when it is helpful for groups to fast together, such as when a congregation is going through difficult times or a mission organization needs to see a substantial breakthrough. In the history of the church there has always been a significant place for fasting together in groups. It is encouraging to be part of a team, as well as the wider body of Christ. National fasts, priestly fasts (i.e., those called by a priest or a leader of a faith community), tribal fasts (as in the Old Testament where an extended family or clan stand together), or family fasts can all carry a great deal of weight. Fasting can be a powerful form of intercessory prayer.

A significant blessing lies in the preparation itself for the community or group to do a fast. I have prepared groups in this way a number of times, and this book is the result of my having written notes for such training years ago. One should be careful not to expect too much too soon from the group, however. You also need to make sure that folks do not get caught up in a group fast when they are not ready to begin fasting.

On the other hand, such fasts can be a very good introduction to fasting for those who have never done it before. They discover the challenges and benefits of fasting in a supportive way. Many people never would have thought of fasting had they not first been part of a group where they discovered the power of fasting.

Longer Group Fasts

The range of options for a group fast is extensive. Are you all going to fast at the same time, or are you setting up a rotation? If you are going to do a water-only fast, are there some who need to do a partial fast for health reasons? Is this an open-ended fast until a goal is achieved, or are you fasting for a specifically defined period? These factors must be carefully considered so that the fast is effective and no one feels excluded, but also so that no damage is done to anyone's health. Pastoral support should be available, especially for those who have not fasted before.

When we did our first workshops in Rwanda in 2006, our church set up a rotation of two people fasting (water-only) for twenty-four hours at a time. This was clearly a significant part of the success of the trip.

You might want to practice various kinds of abstinence in a group setting. For instance, one person might abstain from watching TV, another might go without coffee, and another might get up an hour early to pray. But you commit to the fast together and report back to each other on your progress and battles.

If the group is abstaining from various things, it is important to know what each person is agreeing to do. Write this information down and see that everyone has a copy of it. Make sure that all are honored, regardless of their chosen type of fast. In setting goals, outline the conditions for ending the fast so that everyone is aware of what they are aiming at and what is to happen as they end the fast.

An extended or open-ended group fast is particularly demanding. I have been involved in such an undertaking several times: for example, to intercede for financial provision or for healing for a member of the church injured in a car accident. If there are, say, seven of you fasting, each of you might commit to fasting one day a week and assume that would not be too demanding. But beware—fasting one day a week for six months will drain you significantly, not because of the physical demands but because of the spiritual exhaustion caused by the battle you are engaging.

Long-term fasts need to be well regulated. Goals need to be set precisely and owned by everyone who wants to be involved. The group needs to stay connected either by meeting together in person or by communicating via the Internet. Also, the leader of the group must be fully satisfied that none of those participating will be harmed by fasting. If you have doubts about some individuals, then suggest they check with their doctor first.

Be aware that asking a whole group to fast can be difficult, as I found once when my business was in trouble and all the directors began a fasting rotation. In some cases the lack of food can impact both performance and temperament! But I know of no better way than group fasts to introduce someone to the power of fasting.

In Summary

Learning the discipline of fasting will be a unique journey for all of us. We must each take responsibility for carefully choosing the most appropriate type of fast. If we do too much too soon, it will perhaps detract from other priorities in our lives and hinder rather than release God's purposes as we grow in Christ.

Are you someone who is given to extremes? If so, beware of jumping into too much fasting too quickly. Sometimes the sacrifice of fasting attracts people for the wrong reasons, especially those who struggle from time to time with issues of self-hatred. Try to follow the suggestions of this chapter, starting with occasional short fasts.

For some of us a short water-only fast would be little sacrifice, while turning off the TV, radio, and stereo for twenty-four hours would be a significant challenge. Likewise, deciding to abstain from going dancing is not a fast when you hate dancing anyway! Once you have made a decision regarding the type of fast you are going to try you are then able to decide whether you are going to do this simply as an act of obedience to the Lord or to see some specific need met. Let us turn now to the first category, that which I call a "fast to the Lord."

FASTING TO THE LORD

A common scenario of fasting in Scripture is that of a last resort, sometimes even a panicked response (1 Kings 21:27, 1 Samuel 31:13, Zechariah 8.18–19). Over seventy times in Scripture we see references to fasting. But few of those fall into the category that I have come to call a "fast to the Lord." By this I mean a fast that has no goal other than to focus on the Lord. Such a fast is intended simply to deepen our relationship with Him.

I began doing this type of fast when I was in my teens. It is a fast borne out of a deep desire to know Christ better, to see life from His perspective, and to commune with Him in a more relaxed and gracious way. I would encourage everyone to undertake this type of fast, as it is an excellent way of learning the discipline.

This isn't a fast with a specific goal, such as defeating the Enemy, raising a sum of money, or winning a city for Christ. It is about God and me—just the two of us. I am saying something very fundamental in my fast to the Lord: that He is more important to me than food and my personal well-being.

At one time I would have attributed this kind of fast to the flush of the first love of a new Christian. But on several occasions over the years I have needed to get back in line with the Lord through the discipline of a fast. This has never failed to sort out the matter. At times I have found myself needing to take back ground or maybe reassess where I have reached. In one instance, having experienced a very difficult situation in a local congregation, I found myself needing to take some time off from church to review my position with the church and its leaders.

Types of Fasts to the Lord

The length of such a fast is as long as a piece of string. You may find yourself with a week off work and the need to regroup spiritually. You may choose something intermittent over an extended period of time. Or your fast to the Lord may be short and focused. And the length of the fast may be set for you—either until you have seen the breakthrough you seek or until you have to get back to other duties.

The length and nature of the fast depends on your goals and circumstances. You may have a general desire to grow, or you may know there is something the Lord wants to say but not know what it is. Alternately, you may be having a personal faith crisis of sorts following a tragedy or a reversal of circumstances. Or maybe you just feel jaded in your walk with the Lord. Fasting is an effective means to find faith again and give yourself the time to recover.

You need to ask yourself if you are going to abstain from food or if you are going the non-food route. And will your circumstances allow you to be up and down emotionally, like a yo-yo, or will you be fulfilling a busy lifestyle while you are fasting? The answers to these questions will help guide you through the choices you have to make.

Again, the answer can be simpler than might at first appear. If you are an experienced faster then you can move ahead with all the options on the table. But if you have not had much experience, then you need to operate on the principle of going slow as you proceed.

Choosing a Declaration of Denial That Suits You

If the ultimate goal of your fast is to deepen your faith in Christ, to get to know Him better, or to lift the tarnish from your faith, then a number of options exists to suit you. I have practiced several methods over the years. Missing lunch, doing an exercise program, and praying was a helpful discipline and a declaration to the Lord. Likewise, doing study during my evenings was another big sacrificial declaration.

In the long run you may find that the greatest sacrifices you can make will be giving your time or giving yourself to the Lord in ways that inconvenience you. The so-called spiritual disciplines are the first port of call in getting to know the Lord better: Scripture, prayer, fellowship, study, and others. Anything that helps you focus chiefly on the Lord will be among your first array of choices.

In time you may want to balance this with some food denial as well: for example, taking time every day to meditate on Scripture, combined with drinking juices instead of eating solid food; or instead of eating lunch, studying one of the books of the Bible, combined with a twenty-minute jog.

Although fasting to the Lord is not a goal-oriented fast involving a huge task, it may still help you to think through what you are intending to do and what you want to achieve. But be sure to make Christ the focus. After all, this is a fast to the Lord.

On one occasion when I was going through a rough time with some Christian leaders I committed myself to the task of getting up early and learning all I could about the times, both inside and outside of Scripture, that Jesus is mentioned or described. I discovered that there is more evidence for Christ having lived on the earth than there is for Julius Caesar. But I also met the Lord as I studied and thought about Him.

What Could Happen When We Fast to the Lord?

Meeting the Lord stands head and shoulders above all other experiences and outcomes, especially when it means knowing His actual presence. Not that I have ever presumed on this, and it has only happened a few times in fifty years, but I have known it. Through these incidents I have became aware of how close spiritual reality is to our world. They are within each other in a way that I cannot easily describe. In these moments I realized the Lord was more eager speak to me than I was willing to listen to Him. It was on one such occasion that I began to hear His voice in a new way, a way that has stayed with me ever since.

Either during a fast, much of which can be very barren, or shortly after a fast, I have also found myself thinking thoughts that are new to me. For instance, I began to see from what the Lord was teaching me that human wisdom, as we so often describe it, is not always how God sees things.

One time this lesson came through to me quite forcefully: when I thought I had a matter figured out, the Lord vigorously contradicted my assumptions. This moment was a tipping point for me—because I thought I understood, but the Lord's perspective was the opposite of mine. As a result, when I think I know something I now have a habit of asking myself what the opposite might be, and whether this could be the Lord's perspective. We can be so arrogant about what we think we know and about how we think God views a situation.

Other fasts weren't about great and marvelous things for me to learn, but rather about how God saw me. I had to accept, and confess, issues of sin and deceit in both my personal life and my relationships. I went into one such fast being upset with the Lord and came out most remorseful. I began the fast, to my shame, with an arrogant attitude; and the fast brought me to the foot of the Cross. I found a deeper repentance than I had experienced before.

This steep learning curve has been going on all of my Christian life—that is, seeing things unravel that I didn't even know needed to be unraveled. What all of this has taught me is that we will never fully understand God, but we will never even comprehend His love for us. And we will never have enough wisdom to be able to converse with Him in the way that we really desire.

I had a defining moment in my life during one fast. I heard the Lord speak my name, saying that He loved me. What a deep shock this was, knowing that *He knew me*—that is, that I was loved by Him, for He had called me by name. What more is there in life than to know and experience this, that I am loved by God?

So most of my fasts to the Lord, regardless of how they were planned or organized, usually turned out the same way: me needing to silence myself before the Living God, and in being silenced to listen to what He feels and thinks about matters. Put another way, it is seeing things from an entirely new perspective. Much of my prayer times these days is dedicated to just listening, as I have learned I have very little to say that is useful. His Word is life; so often, sadly, my words are not.

In Summary

What I am suggesting is that you do not need to move the earth in your fasting. Your journey of fasting could, like mine, begin with "selfish" fasts in which you just want to be with the Lord in His presence.

I know that God has set up a veil to prevent us from trespassing into spiritual reality without being invited, but through fasting to the

Lord I have known this veil to be lifted (see 2 Corinthians 3:7–18). None of us has any greater reason to fast than to meet the Lord, one way or another.

Part 2

THE PRACTICE OF FASTING

In this part of the book, I will focus on learning how to fast. The initial guidelines are applicable to all types of fasts. In Part 3, I will address principles that apply specifically to water-only fasting.

BEGINNING YOUR FASTING JOURNEY

I am going to assume two things: 1) that you are new to the spiritual discipline of fasting, but 2) that you are considering beginning a journey of your own. If you are more experienced, I believe you will still find the information in this part of the book helpful in enhancing your spiritual pilgrimage.

I would describe fasting as an act of self-denial that can bring a wide range of benefits to you and to others. It is a powerful weapon in the Kingdom of God for achieving His purposes and for transforming your life and the lives of those who are the focus of your fast. I see fasting as taking authority and responsibility in the spiritual realm for people, needs, and situations.

Sometimes your fasting will target global issues, but this is rarely where any of us start. Cutting our teeth in this discipline often means fasting for what feels mundane. Don't be tempted to take on major battles if you are young in this discipline. Start by learning how fasting affects you and how to manage the impact of its side effects. Don't underestimate the power of small changes to knock you off balance or to jolt your relationships.

It is important to make peace with the fact that Scripture doesn't promote a mechanical approach to the discipline of fasting (for example, fasting for financial provision and getting the money twenty-four hours later). At some points in the church's history or a nation's history a regular routine of fasting has been observed, such as national days of prayer and fasting. Though I am not at all suggesting that this is bad, this shouldn't be the only way for us to see fasting or for us to approach the discipline. Instead, setting aside a perfunctory approach to its practice, I believe fasting is one of those things that we learn by doing. And by doing we begin to write a unique history with the Lord and others.

Fasting should not be entered into as a discipline just because it is found in the Bible or because a book like this recommends it. Having been informed about what Scripture has to say, fasting is then far more of a personal journey. We're not talking about a set of rules that, when followed, delivers certain benefits. Fasting has to do with our relationship with the Lord, not with a formula.

Fasting will be different for everyone, and each person will have a different experience. I have known people who have fasted for two or three days and needed a week to recover. Others have fasted for ten days and never had a complaint. We need to avoid implying that our experience alone is valid, since each of us is unique.

A Word of Warning

I would like to bring some cautions here to those who are considering fasting. I will outline some of the things we should all take into account when considering such a venture. Many of these cautions apply most significantly to extended water-only fasts. But for some people they will be relevant even in the more modest forms of fasting. Later in the book my wife, Mary, will add some cautions based on her experience of being alongside me in my extended fasts.

Fasting, along with many other traditional values like community, equality, and friendship, is becoming more and more fashionable. It has become popular again in the church.[1] As both a spiritual discipline and a health tool in the ever-widening plethora of alternatives to conventional medicine, fasting is increasingly on the agenda. Although I don't pretend to be an expert in healthy living, I have had to learn a lot about my body: what is healthy and not so healthy in my eating and lifestyle and how the discipline of fasting can best be practiced. But I am not primarily taking the health route, since others already have.[2] Instead, my main focus in this book is on fasting "to the Lord"—the idea that we can significantly affect knowing Christ and His perspective through the discipline of fasting.

Please note another key distinction. Fasting as a congregation or a team is a very different exercise than fasting as an individual. As a group you are an army, perhaps modest in size, but nonetheless standing together. Those involved will feel some of the impact and all of the benefit. Just having done it together will be a victory in and of itself. But in a private fast you are an isolated warrior who is seeking to survive. You will feel all of the impact and perhaps see little of the immediate outcome. You are participating, in a real sense, in the death of Christ, especially in an extended water-only fast.

Fasting is not for the proud or arrogant. If you try to fake it—having a pharisaic pretense of fasting when, in fact, you may not be fasting—you could find yourself grieving the Lord with your deceit. Fasting is a deeply

---

1 To illustrate this, go to Google or another Internet search engine and do a search for "Fasting" and "Christianity" to see the endless stream of articles, books, and references on the subject.

2 See, for example, Don Colbert, *Toxic Relief: Restore Health and Energy Through Fasting and Detoxification* (Lake Mary, FL: Siloam Press, 2003).

serious matter and should not be entered lightly. I see the discipline as holy ground we stand on with the Lord. Once or twice in the past I have treated fasting irreverently and suffered for it, having to break the fast with an accompanying humiliation and disconnection of spirit. The very nature of fasting both needs to and should produce a quiet humility, a self-humbling through the denial of food or other comforts. Fasting should humble the spirit of those who enter it correctly, but it can hurt those who do it in pride (see Proverbs 8:12–21; 25:6–8; 29:23).

Another caution about fasting is that it will affect those around you. Although fasting may be practiced in private, it will still impact your immediate circle, especially your family. For instance, my wife has said that I should go away when I am doing extended fasts, as my fasting makes her feel ill as well! Friends and work colleagues will also feel the emotional and spiritual slipstream of what you are doing.

My warning to you is that there is no glory here on earth when you are fasting. The battle is deeply private, and by instinct you will likely not want to share it with anyone except those standing with you in the fast. When you fast you stand alone: weak, vulnerable, and exposed. Don't be tempted to pretend it is any different. I have made it a rule not to talk to anyone outside my immediate support circle regarding what I am thinking or feeling while fasting. This is partly because I have said things I later regretted, but also because as you are going through spiritual and emotional peaks and valleys, it is not helpful for people to get dumped on when you are down or be expected to rejoice with you when you are in the heavens.

On the other hand, it is essential that your fasting includes a relational component. Although it is a very solitary discipline, you must walk the road with others if you are to fast successfully. Talking with others at every stage is a healthy balance to any extremism on your part and helps remove any inverted arrogance. I have been very careful whom I talk to, normally erring on the side of not saying anything. But I have always had one or two people walking the road with me, and I have shared with them even my most intimate thoughts while on a fasting journey.

Adopting a Strategy

As any homebuilder will tell you, the success of a construction project is in the preparation. Whether it is pouring a foundation, or even writing a sermon or planning a vacation, preparation is critical. Once you start the enterprise it quickly becomes evident whether or not you have prepared well. A construction project well done, a sermon effectively delivered, or returning home having enjoyed a well-planned vacation all speak for themselves. Preparation is 90 percent of the battle.

Likewise, it is important to prepare thoroughly for a fast. You are engaging your health and your body, which should be done with the utmost care.

You may find it helpful to read through this whole book before you begin your fast. Once you get into the fast you may find that it is too late to change things. You should be on target before the arrow leaves the crossbow. Time frames, including breaking the fast slowly, are very important.

It is essential that you start small and cautiously. This means having short fasts and manageable goals and not denying yourself something that you feel you simply could not live without. If you start too gently, you can always do another fast that is more challenging. But starting in a manner that is too demanding, so that you feel that you failed in your fast, is a demoralizing way to learn a new spiritual discipline.

If you're doing a food-related fast, I suggest that you first deny yourself addictive foods and snacks for a specific period of time. When you have adjusted to this, do a short fast—perhaps four hours, missing one meal. You might want to repeat this several times in order to learn how you react. You may then want to increase this to an eight-hour fast, then to twelve hours, and then to a one-day, water-only fast.

Most people underestimate the impact that abstaining from food will have on their temperament and body. Most of us need several years of practicing these short fasts before being able to go further. I could not have done my extended fasts without being willing to go through this painful learning curve.

The length of the fast is not that important. What is important is the significance of the denial to you personally. A three-day fast for one person will be as big of a battle as a twelve-day fast for another. I have never regretted doing a fast. But my history in fasting has been a private history. In practice, the time frames are not essential. But the suffering and obedience that accompanies fasting will always be vital, both to the Lord and to you.

The Power of Addictions

All of us are somewhat dependent upon certain routines in our lives that from someone else's perspective could be viewed as addictions. I am not referring to pathological addictions, such as addictions to alcohol, drugs, tobacco, or gambling. We tolerate, almost unknowingly, a number of more subtle addictions. Ingesting caffeine, watching TV, and shopping are some of the most common.

There are three levels of addiction. First, there is the biological level. Coffee and tea, or chocolate, can be eliminated merely by removing them from our diet. Part of your strategy in learning how to fast will be to undo these so-called soft addictions so that they don't distract you from the main purposes of the fast.

Below the biological level lies the emotional addiction or attachment. Most people see the foods and beverages they depend upon in comfort terms—that is, as a way of being nice to themselves or proving to themselves that they are in control. Witness the passionate way some people consume their first cup of coffee in the morning or stop for their favorite snack, telling themselves that their blood sugar is low. Likewise, turning off the TV or radio might create a silence that is noticeably uncomfortable, or even frightening.

The third level, the social/relational aspect, may be the least obvious. But just note how one person going to the coffee machine will cause others from the office to congregate. Or when you stop to make a cup of tea, you feel you need to make a cup for everyone. Addiction becomes acceptable when shared. We transgress together! Don't underestimate this social aspect, as it will likely represent a real loss to you. Try to find a healthy substitute such as juice or fruit, which allows you to still enjoy the relationships.

In Summary

Preparing for fasting is very important. In some ways the quality of our preparation is an indication to the Lord and to ourselves of how seriously we are treating the fast.

You may be contemplating a specific fast for a specific need. It is all too easy to approach fasting with a semi-righteous arrogance, determined to do whatever is necessary to see God intervene in a situation. I want to caution you about this approach and help you to put fasting in context. Jumping in with a more demanding fast is possible, but I would recommend it only if you feel you must and you're convinced that you have God's permission. Make sure you have fully considered the risks and are willing to stop the fast if at any point its impact is harmful to you or to those around you.

I recommend that you view fasting in the context of the long-term growth of your spiritual life. I could not have fasted for twenty to thirty days, once or sometimes twice a year, if I had not approached fasting as a spiritual discipline that was going to grow over the years as part of my ongoing relationship with Christ. If you take this perspective you will be more willing to start gradually.

You may find that fasting is just for a season in your journey to greater maturity and effectiveness in the Kingdom of God. Or perhaps you will find it continues long-term. Either way, a commitment to care for your body and bring an end to unhealthy subtle addictions will be a helpful discipline.

GETTING READY

I like to think that most of us have moments when we consider the possibility of fasting. Perhaps you have hoped if you ignore the moment long enough it will simply pass by! My practice is to listen to those moments and use them to make a decision about whether to fast. Sometimes I choose to fast, other times I don't. Such a decision is between you and the Lord, though I would expect you to consult with those close to you.

In this chapter I would like to share with you some general guidelines related to preparing for fasting. These steps have helped me grow in the discipline. In time you will find that they become instinctive, and you will adapt them to suit your own fasting journey.

Do You Have God's Permission?

It is critical that we ask the Lord for His support or permission to fast. He will oftentimes be silent, leaving the choice to us. But other times He will tell us not to fast because this is not our battle. When God says no, we should back off immediately. Don't be tempted to be a hero and argue with Him, or He may have to say no in a firmer way.

The Lord has given me a choice in every fast I have done. I could have turned around and walked away, which would have been the end of the matter. For instance, I could have referred a person who came to me for help to someone else. Other times I have said yes to the person, but then the Lord has said no. On other occasions the matter has gotten resolved as I was preparing, so I could call the fast off. But if I believed God was in the situation at the beginning, then I was choosing to stand with Christ in the matter to change it through the intervention of my own abstinence.

I had one situation where permission from the Lord came several years before I actually fasted. I made a commitment to pray for Susan Williams, to carry her spiritual healing. I felt a mandate from the Lord to do all I could to see this happen. The initiative was the Lord's, but the timing of the fast was mine. The Lord was faithful in helping me set the agenda for praying for her so that I could then be faithful myself in accepting this mandate from the Lord, but in my own time. *Letting God Heal* tells the full story.[1]

Be careful not to be flattered by the challenge of the need. Be sure the battle is for you. The Lord has used Luke 14:31–33 on many occasions to warn me not to fight every battle in which the Enemy seeks to engage me. In this parable, a king knew he could not win a battle against an opposing king, so he made peace until he was strong enough to take on the enemy. The Devil and his hordes want to wear us down with incessant and un-winnable small skirmishes. In most instances, we should assume the conflict is not for us unless we have special guidance or permission

---

3   S. B. Williams and P. R. Holmes, *Letting God Heal: From Emotional Illness to Wholeness* (Bletchley, UK: Authentic Media, 2004).

from the Lord to take it on. The Lord's advice is that we should wait until we are stronger, until we know we can win this battle

If you are just learning to fast it is not as relevant to ask for God's permission, because the focus of your fast is not so much a significant battle but rather a growing of your own spiritual discipline and muscles. Nonetheless, be alert for when God might tell you not to fast. It is important you know that you and God are in agreement about the fast you are about to undertake. You will need that assurance when you begin to fast and things get difficult.

What Are Your Goals?

Whatever type of fast you choose—abstaining from food or TV, stopping credit spending, getting up earlier to spend time with the Lord, or any other fast—part of the significance of the fast is determined not by what you deny yourself but by why you do it. So when you are considering a fast you will find it very helpful to clearly identify your reasons for fasting. In fact, part of the discipline of fasting is being explicit about what you are seeking from the Lord. What is such a priority for you that you are willing to deny yourself and touch the suffering of a fast in order to see it achieved? Without clear goals you will not be able to tell when your intentions have been met.

The purpose of fasting is as broad as people are different. We all must choose for ourselves whether, why, and how we will fast. I have been amazed, over the years, at the variety of reasons for which people fast. I won't pretend to cover all the options, but I would say that all of them generally fall into the category of either a needs-based fast or a fast to the Lord. Often we will start the idea of a fast with one reason and then find additional reasons later. By the time we actually get into fasting we will normally have a wide range of good reasons. In addition to not having just one clear goal, neither will we normally stay with one goal for the duration of the fast.

Your goals need to be straightforward and unambiguous. If you are fasting for financial provision, and your motives are pure, then your goal is achieved when you see evidence of the receipt of the funds. If you are fasting for knowledge, then carefully write out what you need the Lord to speak to you about. You should be able to state your goal in one or two sentences. It is important that you are able to determine easily whether or not the goal you have set has been met. This will help you learn how to fast more effectively in the future.

When you are fasting to the Lord, the goal is unlike any other. Your purpose may simply be to deepen your relationship with God, to move into greater obedience, or to learn the discipline of fasting. You may sense a clear need to stand with Christ but be unable to articulate why. Though this type of fast often has a less precise goal, you still need to give careful thought to it.

In the past I have suggested to some people that they fast for no other reason than to focus on the Lord or to show that they are really serious about entering such suffering for Him. These are more than adequate goals for a fast, although I would not recommend them as goals for an extended fast until you are experienced enough to know what you are committing to by fasting.

When you are learning to fast, don't be surprised if identifying your goals is a significant challenge. The very act of considering the possibility of fasting means the battle is underway. You might decide to fast prematurely, without carefully considering the goals. Alternately, you might have a clear sense of your goals but mistrust your perspective about fasting, so then delay getting started. This battle eases with practice.

As you outline the possible goals for a fast, sometimes you will find it becomes clear that you really don't need to fast. Perhaps there is other action you should take before considering fasting.

Get It in Writing

Since I began fasting as a teenager I have never begun a fast without writing out word for word the goals for the fast. The only exception has been when I have fasted out of obedience, with no other goal in mind.

I have never seen fasting as a way of storming God's throne and manipulating Him through my suffering. For one thing, such tactics don't work with God. I do enter a fast, however, believing that I have God's agreement for the purpose of my fast, and that it is reasonable and realistic. I then know that by doing the fast I will be guaranteed, one way or another, of receiving my declared goal. Going into the fast with submissive obedience will help assure success.

I don't always know how long the fast will last nor the length of time the answer may take. This has all been an exercise of faith. But what I am suggesting in a sense is, ideally, you are claiming the answer to your specific goal before you actually begin the fast.

Consider Your Addictions

During the preparation stage you need to think about your most vulnerable areas. Do you need to stop drinking coffee and/or tea? Just going through caffeine withdrawal may take several days. For some that can be a fast in itself.

If you are planning to do a non-food fast, are there things you need to do before you begin? For instance, if you are going to abstain from watching TV and you are hooked on certain programs, do you need to stop watching them immediately? And what about other family members watching them, perhaps in another part of the house? If you are going to abstain from food, will you still carry the responsibility of providing the rest of the family a balanced diet? Are there eating habits that you need to break before you even begin to fast?

What about Your Family?

The attitude of your immediate family will likely influence both the type of fast you do and its length. Don't underestimate this important issue. It is particularly essential that well before you undertake an extended water-only fast you inform those close to you that you are thinking of fasting. They may not understand what denial really means, both to you and to them. Such a decision may not mean much to a young child until you don't turn up for meals. So in your decision making you need to take into account how the people you live with will react.

The altered routines of a non-food fast could also bring disruption to your home. Your getting up early, taking up space to study, or keeping the TV turned off could easily affect others. Imposing your fast on them will not be appreciated!

Your family may support your plans wholeheartedly. But on the other hand you might meet some resistance. Perhaps the timing of your fast doesn't suit them or the type of fast poses a problem for them. Your family may be worried they will be a target of the Enemy because of your spiritual initiative. If you sense the Lord calling you to fast, you should seek your family's support and find a way to conduct your fast so that it has minimal impact on them. But if you have difficulty gaining their support, then you need to seriously consider putting your plans on hold.

Let's assume that you have won the support of your family. You must now include them in your preparation. If you have young children, then it might be better for you to go away rather than to disrupt household routines—especially if you would be a grumpy old bear. While it is important to communicate to those close to you about your fast, you must do this in such a way that you don't come across as a hero, on one hand, or that they will not be able to count on you, on the other hand.

I hold to the principle that I must help maintain routines as much as I can. For example, when I am on a water-only fast I still sit at the table during meals, and I often even cook the meal. Although this may seem to defeat the purpose of freeing up mealtimes for things like prayer, it may be helpful to join the family at mealtimes for the sake of your children. During an extended fast from TV you might make an exception of watching a favorite program or a movie with your children on occasion. Don't disrupt the routines of others more than you must.

Who Will Support You?

As you prepare to fast, ask yourself who will be your confidante supporting you on your journey. The bigger the fast, the more important it will be to have someone in that capacity. Be careful not to choose a person who is rarely available and is therefore difficult to meet with or talk to on the telephone.

This need is significant particularly if you are single and don't have the support of a spouse. If you have housemates, you should tell them what you are doing. Beyond that, make sure there is someone sharing with you in the battle you are undertaking.

If you are married, your spouse should be fully informed of your fast, though it is not always appropriate to have him or her be the only person who is standing with you. If your fast is related to your work or business and your spouse is not integrally involved, it would be helpful to have at least one other person walking with you. Or if you are fasting *for* your spouse, it is important to have someone else standing with you for further support.

Weather, Travel, and Schedules

We move on now to some practicalities. Weather, travel plans, and your schedule will be key factors in deciding whether to fast and for how long you are able to do so.

If you are planning to abstain from food during the winter, especially if you live in a cold part of the world, is your home comfortably warm? Can you take a hot bath? (A shower just doesn't do it!)

Will you be doing a lot of traveling? If so, that's not the best time for most people to fast from food. If you will be driving, will the car be comfortable if you are not eating?

You must take schedule commitments into account. I often waited until I had space in my date book before God gave me permission to begin an extended fast. On occasion I was able to clear my calendar. Consider your upcoming commitments. Do you have a particularly demanding engagement or project scheduled? This may not change your decision to fast, but it may affect the timing or the nature of the fast.

One way of planning ahead is by not accepting dinner dates during the time you will not be eating. This will also spare you from admitting, when you arrive, that you are fasting!

In Summary

In the process of getting ready to fast, one key question remains: How do we decide what type of fast to do? We must identify what we are abstaining from and how long we plan to do so.

We talk in our ministry about God "turning up the volume," as well as about us "turning up the volume" in response to circumstances. Your decision will be a combination of your own experience and the nature of that for which you are fasting. You don't need a big mallet to crack an egg. Neither should you use a small hammer to try to knock over an oak tree. Once you are an experienced faster the gravity of the situation itself should tell you clearly.

Put another way, what are the criteria for your decision? To get the right answers you must ask the right questions. So prepare carefully. And if you can, talk things through with others. What would an appropriate response be to the challenge you are facing? Would you be overreacting if you did a particular fast? How does your date book look? What are your family commitments? What spiritual tools do you need in order to do this job?

For most of us the first question is whether to abstain from food or something else. If you are new to fasting, you may determine that you need to start by abstaining from something other than food while you tackle some of your soft addictions. If you decide to do a water-only fast, and it is your first one, then it is advisable to keep it short. This allows you to grow into the pathway of fasting.

On the other hand, if you are fasting from something other than food, be careful to choose wisely. Avoid the temptation to use fasting to manipulate other members of your family to change their behavior. Guard against arrogance or pride about what you are doing.

Finally, as we have already noted there is no doubt that abstaining from food is more demanding than other forms of denial. And an extended fast raises the stakes even higher for you and for everyone around you. Experience will help pave the way to making right decisions.

Let us assume that you have made your decision and are now on your fast. What should you be doing during the fast?

9.

DURING YOUR FAST

While preparing for a fast it is quite common to feel you have already started. You are already beginning to engage the issues. Nonetheless, there will be a noticeable change the moment your fast actually begins. How you conduct yourself during a fast obviously contributes to its effectiveness and overall success.

Keeping a Journal

I have kept a journal for most of my fasts, from the shortest to the longest (thirty-nine days). In these accounts I have been able to track much of the emotional helter-skelter of the daily battles: unexpected pressures, failures, defeat, pain, and ultimate victory.

I can still smell the spring rains through some of the pages. I remember the sea mist drifting in early in the morning, the joy of cooking spaghetti Bolognese for Mary and Christopher (my wife and son), and leaving the office pretending I was going out for lunch or supper like everyone else.

You keep a journal as part of your prayer journey, as part of the intercession, as part of your hope and declaration that you are going to reach the end and use the knowledge, money, or sacrifice as God wished. It helps you to prepare for how you will use the new freedom or the deeper intimacy with Christ for which you long.

I believe it is important that you write extensive notes on what you are thinking and feeling. During a water-only fast most people develop a level of awareness of themselves, especially of their own body, they have not had before. Despite the pain in your body you are able, in a somewhat twisted way, to sense more around you. Color can seem more intense during fasts. Sounds can appear sharper. Worship, especially, has deeper meaning. Relationships become more important to you. Some of the most obvious and profound things I have learned from the Lord have come during these seasons. Record all of this in your journal.

But also write about the dark moments: the evenings consumed by dreaming of breaking your fast, followed by going to bed committed to breaking the fast in the morning, then getting up and wondering what all the fuss was about.

If you are doing a non-food fast and studying or spending more time listening to the Lord, then taking some of this time to write journal notes would be a natural. The most important element of your journaling is monitoring your progress and looking for breakthroughs. The more you build up your practice of fasting the more these records become a testimony to the effectiveness of your obedience and to the supernatural intervention of God.

Christ Anoints What He Gives

Having identified your goals, as we discussed in the previous chapter, you are now living them. You are carrying them by faith in your spirit. The fast becomes a way of believing they will be achieved. We need to begin dreaming about what it will be like when we have what we are seeking.

Focus on your goals routinely during the fast. Part of the consequence will be that in God's provision we can also see His anointing. Those He calls He also equips. Put simply, if the Lord asks you to dig a hole He will provide the shovel. He will provide His anointed blessing for you to move easily into the new open space to which He is leading you.

Record in your journal your changing thinking regarding the goals and what you are beginning to believe about the outcome. Live and breathe as though the outcome is already on its way.

For a long time I had a sense that I would one day have permission from the Lord to write some of what He has been teaching me since the early 1960s. But I needed a publisher that was interested. Following a fast one came, together with the provision to write. I now have a dozen books in print.

Likewise, when I needed knowledge to help a certain person who was close to me, I received it as I was fasting. And I was also given wisdom to know how and when to share this with the person.

Expectations about Hearing from God

I have met very few people who have done fasts and experienced God speaking to them a lot during those times. For me, the period of fasting is, instead, usually a time of spiritual barrenness. The heavens feel like brass. When beginning an extended fast I usually find myself saying goodbye to the Lord, because He will probably not talk to me for some time to come.

God's voice brings life to us, which can go against the spirit of self-denial of a fast. So when we enter into even a short time of self-denial it should not surprise us that we lose this. I realize this is not always the case. Some people have a spiritual high. Derek Prince, for example, said that was what he expected.[1] But this has not been my experience, so you should be prepared for silence rather than seeing fasting as a more intimate time the Lord.

I have come to learn that there are a number of reasons why the Lord may be silent. He could be testing your mettle. He could be waiting. He could be unable to say anything until you are a little weaker and more vulnerable in spirit. But one thing is certain: there is a good chance you will experience darkness and barrenness, for fasting is bringing a kind of dying on yourself, thereby helping you to enter more deeply the sufferings of Christ (Romans 8:17). You are aligning yourself voluntarily and vicariously with the suffering of Jesus. There is nothing the Enemy hates more than being reminded of the finished work of Christ.

There are exceptions to this. During your fast it is likely that you are reading the Bible or books about other Christians' journeys, and in that case you can expect the Lord to talk to you. Or if you are doing a fast to the Lord, then you are deciding to make His voice central, as well as being willing yourself to listen and act on what He says. So choose the type of fast carefully, with the outcome in mind.

So a fast for me is like the still before the storm. It is the calm and quiet before the kids get home. But for other people I talk to fasting is a rich time, a time when they hear a lot from the Lord and things come alive for them.

---

1   Derek Prince, *How to Fast Successfully* (Charlotte: Derek Prince Ministries, 1976), 30ff.

Because most long food fasts have been times of barrenness for me, when I fast I try to keep ministry to a minimum, as the slightest exertion has a tendency to drain my spirit. Keep notes of all that you think and feel. Let the Lord be your friend and guide through this challenging time.

The Role of Scripture

Scripture can and should play a significant role in your fast. Establish a reading plan before you begin, and organize your time so that you can read that portion of God's Word. Make time to refocus on the Lord through Scripture.

I have noted during several of my fasts, however, that my concentration, especially during the first four to seven days, gets lost. Therefore I have found it hard to focus on reading. I had dreams of spending long hours in bed or curled up in my favorite chair reading, but when the opportunity arrived I couldn't focus or concentrate.

I have found meditating on Scripture is helpful for this dilemma. Often I have focused on difficult passages or verses that bothered me. I spent time reading those passages, letting the Lord talk to me about them. I wanted to know His perspective on what was written. What did He intend this to mean to us today? How is it relevant? What should we be doing with this problematic verse or passage? While fasting I have gained some of my deepest insights into the meaning of God's Word and what it teaches us.

This will be particularly relevant when you do a non-food fast and make the focus on the Lord a central part of the fast. And, of course, if you are not eating you have extra time to focus on Him.

I suggest that you begin the day with a passage or a verse and carry it with you through the day. On one occasion I found myself reflecting on the passages where Jesus condemned the arrogance and hypocrisy of the Pharisees (e.g., Matthew 23:27–28). On another occasion I focused on what I would do with the knowledge God gave me as I broke the fast—i.e., what servanthood and humility meant in specific situations. Carry the Word of God into and through your fast.

Feeling the Darkness

Fasting, especially of the extended variety, is a fast-track route to the Enemy's attention. A primary biblical example is the temptation of Jesus (Matthew 4:1–11; Luke 4:1–13). Fasting as an act of surrender to the Lordship of Christ will usually attract the Enemy and his hordes. Some sense this even before beginning a fast, or will know it at different times during the fast. It becomes evident in a number of ways. Before and during fasts I have always felt a lot of death (Philippians 3:10), including mocking from others and the Enemy.

There is a greater physical dimension to the feelings of death as part of a water-only fast. Certain people suddenly turn up and attack you when you are most vulnerable. Some people will not understand your fast, and their attitude can feel like it undermines you even if they have no knowledge of what you are doing. You may also hear and sense things that you know are spiritual, yet they are not from the Lord. This means that the Devil is not far away.

Communicating with Others

Much of what is happening to you will inevitably be very private: between you, the Lord, and those supporting you in the fast. But you must also consider how your fast is going to impact others. While I am fasting, as a general rule I do not talk to people about what is happening to me, what I am learning, or the direction the fast is taking me. The reason for this will be obvious as you begin to fast. At times you will feel miserable and morose. What you say in the midst of such sacrifice might well not be uplifting. So be judicious in what you say even to those close to you. You don't want to regret it later, and neither do you want to negatively impact them. Love those around you with your words; and don't dump on them—do the dumping in your journal.

But since the self-denial and isolation of a fast can easily lead you into an unhealthy form of privacy, it is a helpful practice to keep in touch with those who have agreed to support you in your fast. Be honest with them about how you are feeling and about whether you see your goals being achieved. If they have done some fasting themselves they may be able to offer you advice about the most challenging areas of your fast. Allow them to make constructive comments—for instance, questioning the wisdom of prolonging a fast rather than breaking it.

Do Things You Enjoy

While you are fasting, especially if you are abstaining from food for very long, you will need to slow down in recognition of the fact that you cannot function at your normal pace. It is important, however, that you don't become an ascetic. Don't let the fact that you aren't eating cut you off from your family or your circle of friends.

I have had convertibles much of my life and I love to drive, so when I am fasting I enjoy going for a drive. I also love to go to the beach, so I do that as well. I love to go to the local health club and sit in the Jacuzzi— definitely a heavenly thing to do during a fast! I love to do ministry with people too, so I never cut back completely in my counseling if I know my spirit can sustain it. Likewise, I enjoy teaching and training, so I continue doing some of that through my business and church. Don't allow a fast to segregate you from others and the things you like to do.

There is always a danger that you will be consumed by the denial and darkness that accompanies fasting. You can slip into feeling that there is merit simply in punishing yourself. You might even *try* to punish yourself, in fact. It is important to keep a balance so you are aware that fasting is an act of love for God, for others, and for yourself. Though it is deeply sacrificial, fasting must be fundamentally driven by love rather than by self-affliction.

When a Fast Turns Sour

Sometimes a fast will go wrong. I remember fasting for a day when I was a teenager. As I was sitting at the kitchen table that afternoon I grabbed a cookie out of the cookie jar and ate it before I realized what I had done. I still had a ways to go at that age!

One time I started a fast but then remembered I had a very important lunch date, which I had forgotten to put in my date book. During one fast my wife got quite ill, and on another occasion my son needed some significant support.

It is not uncommon to get sick while fasting. After fasting for two days one time I came down with the flu. I'm sure I felt worse than normal because I was weakened by not eating. Though I continued fasting, the best practice probably would have dictated that I break the fast.

On the other hand, those close to you might get sick or feel unable to continue supporting you. They may even become angry at what they perceive to be selfishness on your part in your fasting. When others begin to suffer too much, then you must break the fast. But be aware that this might be manipulation or jealousy on their part. It may be helpful to discuss this with them as you prepare for your next fast.

On other occasions you might be the problem. You might be acting like a prima donna. If you find that you are behaving like a spoiled child, then you should stop fasting until you can do so with more maturity.

One certainly needs grace and dignity to practice the discipline of fasting successfully. You may need to admit you made a mistake, and perhaps apologize to others as well. I once began a prolonged fast but then got very ill and had to stop. I later saw that I had misjudged the whole spiritual landscape; getting sick was evidence of God's graciousness to me.

In such circumstances you need to break your fast, forgiving yourself along with others for any unhelpful contribution they may have made.

Breaking a Fast Properly

How you break a fast is a surprisingly important and complex topic. Overindulging on food after not eating for a day, binging on TV after not watching for a week, or spending all the money you saved after abstaining from recreational shopping for a month—all of these are an assault on the spirit of the fast that you have just completed. It might sound ridiculous, but you will often be more tempted in retreat than you were in the fast.

Undoubtedly, the type of fast you must be most careful about breaking is one that involves abstinence from food, especially extended water-only fasts. Later in the book I will have more to say about how to end this type of fast. Regardless of its length, breaking a fast is part of the spiritual discipline of fasting.

In any fast, you should hold on to what you learned or gained instead of going back to old patterns. After a fast from television, for example, perhaps you will determine not to turn the TV on until nine in the evening and then turn it off before the late-night shows begin. Don't just slip back into your old routines, or else you will lose part of the fruit of your fast.

An example from my life is that I now only drink, at the most, one cup of coffee a day. My body can handle that most days, though I may go weeks without drinking coffee. Another long-term change is that I eat very little bread, pasta, or potatoes. Being in my sixties, I do not need these high-energy foods. A lifetime of fasting has given my body the ability to work well on a modest intake of calories.

Resolve to break a food fast in a way that honors the Lord and your own body. If you have not eaten for a few days, you should take the same amount of time to break the fast completely. Resist the temptation to gorge yourself.

Also, don't be hasty to declare that your goals have been achieved. I take more of a "wait and see" approach. When seeking knowledge on someone's behalf I will sometimes meet the person while I am still fasting and share what I believe the Lord has for him or her. I test my perception. If the knowledge you are obtaining has an originality about it, or was not what you expected, then it is likely from the Lord. But if you are thinking thoughts that you could have thought without the fast, then you are probably not there yet. You need to wait for something more unexpected, something supernatural from the Lord.

Most often, however, I fast without that individual knowing I was fasting for knowledge to help him or her. It is a sweet moment when you see your words being aloe on the wound or balm on a troubled spirit, giving the person hope and a way forward.

If you have been mature and discreet about your fast, then coming off it should be easy, as people will just continue to treat you as they did before. Only you and your one or two supporters will really know what has gone on in your life.

Chronicling Your Fast

Write out your thoughts in detail as you reach the end of your fast. Why are you bringing the fast to a close? Why do you feel the way you do? How will you move on with the provision God has given or the decisions you have made? I once ended a fast on the basis of financial provision promised by a person, but then a month or two later that individual denied making the commitment. I was glad I could go back to my notes to prove to myself that I wasn't crazy!

Record the impact the fast has had on both you and your family. What habits were the most challenging to break? If you were fasting from food, note the state of your body and your health. Record your weight. Has the fast affected, for instance, your joints, eyesight, or driving reactions? How do you feel when you get up in the morning? What are the battles at night?

It is helpful not to plunge back into the chaos of daily life. Take time to reflect and write. Reading this again will be useful preparation for your next fast.

In Summary

The spiritual disciple of fasting presents a golden opportunity to make positive changes in our lives. It provides a perfect opening to develop new habits. How you live immediately after a fast is just as important as how you lived during the fast. So seize the opportunity.

The practice of fasting can be quite significant. Breaking an addiction to pornography and placing an auditor or filter on your laptop, as a result of a fast, is a good move. Making a decision to eliminate unhealthy snacks becomes a lifestyle change. Let your fast count for much more than just a brief period of abstinence. Let it change your life.

THE HEALTH BENEFITS OF FASTING

In this book we are focusing on fasts that are a purposeful act of denial in order to achieve specific goals. Fasting from food is practiced in many parts of the world, however, purely on health grounds. For example, many of the health spas in Germany and other parts of Europe practice fasting for health, and in China fasting is regularly practiced as a form of cleansing toxins from the body. In this chapter I want to highlight the physical benefits of short food-related fasts and an ongoing regimen of healthy eating.[1]

Give It a Rest

Think about this: from the time your stomach is formed, in the third to fourth month after conception, until the moment you die, your

---

2   I am indebted to physician Brian McDonogh for his expertise and input in this chapter.

stomach hardly ever gets even one day off! It is virtually always working. Would the people running a factory treat their machinery that way, never giving it a break for service? But that is what we expect from our stomach and digestive system. I realize that none of our other organs that function involuntary (e.g., heart, lungs, liver, kidneys) get a break. The difference with our digestive system, however, is the voluntary dimension of our eating and drinking. Your stomach could have some time off if you would let it!

Your digestive system is a group of organs that expand and contract, continually breaking down the carbon-based material you give it. This process marches on without complaint as you fill your stomach—except when you overfill it, in which case it might get "upset"!

Giving your digestive system a break is a good thing. Your pangs of hunger are not evidence of actual hunger or starvation, but merely your body complaining that it is not getting the next meal on time. This can be a cause of panic for many of us. But "I'm starving!" is not true until we really are, which for most people usually occurs between twenty-five and thirty-five days into a water-only fast.

Fasting allows your overworked digestive system to stop, detox itself, and rest for a while. The infusion of constant food is interrupted, and your body gets a chance to cleanse itself and then rest. Your stomach works 24/7 all of your life, with absolutely no respite unless you decide on it.

While resting during a fast the body will be very active in other ways, however. The main organs for discharging toxins from our bodies are the stomach, colon, kidneys and urinary tract, lungs, and skin. Fasting, especially when followed by a juice regimen, will promote the detoxifying processes of these organs. Adopting such a practice brings some much-needed deep healing to our bodies. For instance, your overburdened liver can do its best work of detoxifying both itself and your blood when it no longer has to cope with food as well. At the same time, your stomach, pancreas, intestines, and gallbladder will get a much-deserved rest.

But the benefits go further. In addition to your blood, your lymphatic system is also effectively cleansed of toxic buildup through fasting. Our cells, tissues, and organs begin to dump the accumulated waste from the cellular metabolic processes of digestion. Let me explain.

All human cells produce waste in the process of digesting nutrients, and the high consumption of food that most of us eat means the body can be overwhelmed by the workload of detoxifying. Fasting, therefore, allows this waste collection process to catch up. As fatty tissue is burned during the fast, chemicals and toxins that would normally be broken down by the liver are released and excreted through the kidneys and the bile.

It is not uncommon during the initial period of an extended fast for boils and skin rashes to appear and for body odor to be emitted through the body's largest excretory organ, the skin. Our bodies are designed to do this, as this detox is programmed into the natural healing cycles of the body. The problem is that most of us don't stop eating long enough to allow this process to take place. In this sense, the spiritual discipline of fasting is healing to our bodies as well as our spirits, allowing our physical cells to cleanse themselves.

Each cell is an energy factory, and one part of the cell is the waste processor, called the mitochondrion. Due to a number of factors within and outside the human body, like metabolic waste, chemicals, and other toxins, the mitochondria within the cells are often overworked. This blocks the body's ability to function well. Fasting is a natural way for the mitochondrion of every cell to recover, thereby releasing new energy at a cellular level. Through the mitochondria the body is programmed during a fast to initiate a deep cleansing of every cell.

So please give serious consideration to the health benefits of fasting. This will be the only opportunity your stomach and digestive tract has to rest. Allow it to do so, and invite the Lord to bring cleansing health to all your organs as they go through this cycle.

Juice Fasts

As I have mentioned, fasting has become popular simply because of its health benefits rather than as an act of intercession. The idea, however, is not the classic water-only fast.

Most of us have bodies that are too acidic (toxic). The typical person's urinary pH reading is around 5.0, when it should be around 6.8 to 7.0. This is actually much worse than it appears, since 5.0 is one hundred times more acidic than 7.0. The more acidic one's urine is, the more minerals are lost. One's cells also become less permeable, resulting in constipation and toxicity.

One of the reasons for this situation is that the body collects, over the years, a variety of contaminants that are not easily excreted through the body. Lead pollution in the atmosphere is a typical example. Lead is a heavy metal that the body absorbs but cannot easily dispel. Our atmosphere and many of the pollutants in it are all acidic in nature, whereas most natural, unprocessed foods are more alkaline in nature. This means that much food is medicine to the body, whereas heavy metals in any form or quantity are usually more toxic to us.

On the basis of such thinking a movement is being birthed that promotes periodic fasting followed by a cleansing diet of natural, organic foods that can help return the pH balance to a healthier norm and cleanse the body of excess toxic nutrients, fats, and chemicals. The regimen would look something like this: You do a water-only fast for, say, three days, which begins the detox process. You then follow this with a juicing fast, which is one of the safest and best ways to flush and heal the body of such toxins.

Claims are also being made that water-only fasting, especially when followed by a juice detox, can also help protect the body against a range of autoimmune diseases, like lupus and rheumatoid arthritis, as well as severe atherosclerosis (such as severe coronary artery disease). Such fasting is also known to reduce inflammation in the body.[2]

"Juicing" typically refers to mixing in a blender a combination of organic raw fruits and vegetables.[3] As well as detoxifying the body, juicing also provides relief for the gastrointestinal tract. The Western world is becoming known for being overfed and undernourished. Juice fasting hearkens back to Greek times, when Hippocrates and others treated the *patient* rather than, as in modern medicine, just the *disease*.

The principle of juice fasting is simple. Our bodies use a lot of energy each day digesting, absorbing, and assimilating food. By juicing fruits and vegetables you allow your body to digest nutrition without a large amount of energy going into the digestive process. Juicing allows the body to get on with detoxifying itself.

Some, following the lead of Peter D'Adamo, would also have us take into account our blood type in determining what foods are good for us to juice and what foods are actually poisonous for our particular blood type.[4] It may be too obvious for words, but we are normally addicted to those foods and habits that harm us the most.

But let's assume you are now deciding on a fast and want to know the best way forward to help you on your spiritual journey while also offering health to your body.

---

1   Don Colbert, *Toxic Relief: Restore Health and Energy Through Fasting and Detoxification* (Lake Mary, FL: Siloam Press, 2003), 51.

2   Personally, I am not a big fan of juicing. Why juice succulent fruits and vegetables that you can masticate in your mouth, getting your digestive juices going, rather than juicing and losing these benefits?

3   Peter J. D'Adamo, *Eat Right 4 Your Type: The Individualized Diet Solution to Staying Healthy, Living Longer and Achieving Your Ideal Weight: 4 Blood Types, 4 Diets* (New York: Putnam, 1996).

The "Daniel Fast"

I call what has become for me a way of life the "Daniel fast." This eating regimen is low in salt, sugar, and "bad fat."[5]

When Daniel, who would become a great Old Testament prophet, was a young man, he was taken into captivity in Babylon and brought into service in the royal palace. He and his three young friends were assigned "a daily amount of food and wine from the king's table" (Daniel 1:5). But Daniel was determined not to "defile himself" with this food (verse 8), probably a reference to the fact that the first portion of it had been offered to idols. Instead, Daniel and his companions ate a diet of vegetables and water.

After ten days of this fare, Daniel and his fellow Israelites "looked healthier and better nourished than any of the young men who ate the royal food" (verse 15). This type of food—simple, unprocessed, and usually organic—has become much more fashionable in recent times, given problems such as obesity and the appalling damage done to food by mass production, deep-freezing, or adding ingredients to extend shelf life.

I now find that my body is best suited to plain foods. My typical diet these days, for both weight control and healing nourishment, consists of lightly steamed vegetables seasoned with garlic and spices, steamed fish several times a week, and plain, grilled chicken or turkey (without the skin). I don't eat much red meat, pork, or dairy products, except for skim milk in tea. I am also guided in this by my blood type in regard to the foods that are most suitable for me.[6]

This approach to diet is then generously supplemented by a wide variety of mostly seasonal, fresh (and inexpensive) fruits, without any

---

4   Some types of fat are good while others are not so good. See William Castelli and Glen Griffin, *The New Good Fat, Bad Fat: Lower Your Cholesterol and Reduce Your Odds of a Heart Attack* (Cambridge, MA: Fisher Books, 1997).

5   D'Adamo, *Eat Right 4 Your Type.*

added sugar. I have come to really enjoy these simple tastes without the sauces, ketchup, or salt. I also rarely eat processed and/or prepackaged foods or anything fried. Together with my power walk every day, I have been able to live healthier than when I ate anything given to me. (Having said this, I do occasionally treat myself to an un-thickened Irish stew or cheese and biscuits.)

I am not saying this regimen is for everyone, but for my type of body it is very healthful. You might need to find a diet plan that suits your body, and then change your eating habits to accommodate it. We all need to gain a greater understanding of what is healthy for the human body in general and our own bodies in particular, so that we can adapt our eating habits and lifestyle accordingly.

Alternately, perhaps you would want to adopt the Daniel fast for a fixed period, maybe a week. It's an option that could readily be incorporated into a very demanding lifestyle or used by someone for whom it is not safe to abstain completely from food.

Healthy Living

It may seem strange to include a chapter on healthy eating in a book on fasting, but I feel it is important. If fasting is to become a regular discipline for you, as it has for me, understanding its impact on your body and how to take care of your body between fasts are fundamental aspects of that discipline.

Interest in the human body and how it works has expanded rapidly in recent times. As a consequence we have a growing knowledge about how the body does and does not cope with things like fast food, stress, addictions, lack of exercise, and obesity. Such information can be helpful as background in establishing ground rules for extended fasting.

Our growing awareness of the needs and function of the human body is leading us to numerous alarming conclusions. One is that we in the Western world are among the most overfed and undernourished people on earth. Our bodies need ample amounts of nutrition, yet most of us eat more and more devitalized foods. Our soils are getting poorer and our foods more processed, so what we eat is becoming less and less nourishing. One of the reasons for this is that we no longer follow the fallow year recommended in Scripture, where we let the ground rest every seventh year (Exodus 23:10–11; Leviticus 25:3–4). But our diet also consists mainly of prepared, processed, and/or fried foods, all of which tend to be low in nourishment and high in unhealthy fats.

We all have two kinds of cholesterol in our body. The "good" one is called high-density lipoprotein (HDL), while the "bad" one is called low-density lipoprotein (LDL). HDL is essential for life, necessary for the formation of cell membranes and steroid hormones like cortisol, testosterone, estrogen, and progesterone. But unhealthy fats—saturated hydrogenated fats and trans-fatty acids—are now killing us with a variety of diseases.[7]

In addition to eating more and more bad fat, because so much of our food is processed and therefore "dead," it is much less nourishing to our bodies. So we tend to gorge ourselves with increasing amounts of food to offset our body's decreased intake of nourishment. Walking away hungry after a meal is a classic sign of this process. In a sense a person is moving into malnutrition. In response to this, some are suggesting we need to return to a diet of the type that Jesus ate.[8]

Another factor also needs to be considered. Many people today realize they are harming themselves by their diet. So they begin taking vitamins and supplements. Most of these, however, are also "dead." I'm not knocking vitamins and supplements, but merely making the point

---

6   In addition to Castelli and Griffin, *The New Good Fat, Bad Fat*, see Robert Povey, *How to Keep Your Cholesterol in Check* (London: Sheldon Press, 2003).

7   Don Colbert, *What Would Jesus Eat? The Ultimate Program for Eating Well, Feeling Great, and Living Longer* (Nashville: Thomas Nelson, 2002).

that it might be easier for our bodies if we ate foods that gave us these benefits naturally rather than expecting our bodies to absorb synthetic substitutes because we cannot be bothered to be more disciplined in our eating.

Instead, we need to change the way we eat: consuming far less fast food, processed food, fried food, unhealthy fat, salt, sugar, and artificial sweeteners. That is, the range of foods we ingest should, on the whole, contribute to the healing and restoration of our bodies. Much of our typical diet does not. For instance, it makes sense that we should eat five portions of fruit and vegetables a day. A portion could be a piece of fruit, a handful of grapes, or the equivalent of a small glass of juice. But how many of us do that?

So before we even begin thinking about fasting, some of us will need to change our lifestyle and our diet. Devitalized, low-nourishment foods will not help heal and restore your body after an extended fast. In fact, eating such foods could help prolong the agony of breaking the fast. The body will not bounce back the way it should if we are not feeding it nourishing foods.

In Summary

Perhaps you will consider eating more healthily as a result of reading this book. But I would go one step further and suggest that times of fasting are healthy for our body. I am not referring to extended fasts so much. But there is clear medical evidence to indicate that, especially for those of us in the West, occasional short water-only fasts bring cleansing to the body. For example, losing just a few pounds, providing you keep it off, can significantly reduce your chances of contracting a multitude of serious diseases.

The fasting we are talking about in this book is not primarily for the purpose of physical health. Nonetheless, you may want to consider a fast specifically for this purpose before engaging in the more demanding spiritual dynamics of fasting. It will help you identify how challenging the physical demands of a fast might be for you. Do be aware, however, of any personal health factors that might make this unwise for you.

Part 3

FASTING FROM FOOD

We will now focus specifically on those fasts
that relate to food. Because they affect our
bodies so directly, they have a far wider range of
consequences and must be handled with care.
I am including the most demanding form of
fasting: extended water-only fasts. Not all of us
are called to them, but I am convinced that their
rewards in the Kingdom of heaven are significant.
It is my prayer that God will raise up an army
of those able to undertake this type of fasting,
together with their supporters, to prepare the
church for the last days.

HEALTH WARNING

As we tackle the topic of water-only fasts, I want to remind you again of the health warning:

Please note that this is not a medical textbook on fasting but a handbook intended to introduce the subject to Christians who may be interested in exploring this discipline. Before you consider fasting it may be advisable to talk to a health care professional. This is especially important if you are taking medication or have a history of illness. Neither the author, the publisher, nor any of their affiliates can be held responsible for any outcomes if you do decide to fast to the Lord.

11.

CONSIDERING A WATER-ONLY FAST

We move now to the topic of water-only fasting, the practice most commonly associated with the word *fasting*. Due to its direct and immediate physical effects, such fasting must be undertaken cautiously. The more understanding you have, the more successful your fast is likely to be. The things you need to do to prepare for denying yourself food will eventually become instinctive and routine. But to start with it is best to do them very carefully and deliberately.

Medical Cautions

If you could harm your body by doing a water-only fast, you must seriously question whether the Lord is giving you permission to do such a fast. Under such circumstances, the other types of fasts—a non-food fast, a juice fast, or a Daniel fast—would be more pleasing to Him.

If you suffer from any kind of stomach disorder or digestive tract problem, or if you have suffered damage to the lining of your stomach in the past, you should definitely reconsider the prospect of water-only fasting. Merely emptying your stomach may quickly expose any problem with your stomach or digestive tract. Before you attempt to fast, talk to your doctor to determine if you need to find a form of self-denial other than abstaining from food.

When you begin to fast and there is no food in your stomach, there will be a period of time in which your stomach continues the digestive cycle by creating digestive acids. For most of us this creates a significant buildup of acid in the stomach, causing our pH balance to become more acidic. This part of a fast will be agony if you already have damage to your stomach or digestive tract. In any case, be cautious in your first fasts as you move into this part of the cycle.

Fasting is also generally more difficult for those whose daily lives involve physically demanding activities, for those who have a high rate of metabolism, and for those who are going through hormonal change. Women need to take into account the ramifications of their monthly cycle. If a woman is pregnant or breast-feeding, she will likely want to choose a fast that does not involve abstinence from all food, and definitely not a fast that involves abstinence from water.

If you are on medication, especially to treat a medical condition like diabetes, you need to talk to your doctor before doing a water-only fast for longer than one day. In the case of many oral medications it is assumed that you are eating normally, as the medication is designed to break down in the stomach along with food and liquids. This is just as true with timed-release or sustained-release drugs. Although they release their medication more slowly, the assumption that you will have food in your stomach still applies.

It is not wise to take any medication on an empty stomach. Even diluting some medications in water doesn't stop them from damaging the lining of the stomach. Again, if you have any questions or concerns about fasting in light of your medication, please seek professional advice.

Soluble aspirin can cause bleeding of the stomach lining, so if you need to take a pain reliever while fasting you may want to use enteric-coated aspirin or acetaminophen (e.g., Tylenol). Other types of anti-inflammatories, such as ibuprofen (e.g., Advil and Motrin), may also prove useful for headaches, even intense ones. I have gotten bad headaches for no apparent reason during a water-only fast. The right side of my head and my forehead are the two areas where I seem to feel empathetic pain.

The issue of containing and managing pain should be taken very seriously. Don't try to be a hero and tough it out. I have always given myself permission to take pain medication during a fast if the pain gets unbearable. But I would recommend dissolving the medication in a glass of water so that it doesn't concentrate in your stomach. And remember that since you are taking it on an empty stomach it works much more quickly. I have felt a rush within minutes.

Disorders and Addictions

Anorexia and bulimia are of particular concern, since fasting can be a way of promoting the worst aspects of these disorders. Asking someone with anorexic tendencies to fast could be a gift! Anyone currently struggling with an eating disorder should not fast, and anyone who has a history of such disorders should only fast with caution—making a commitment to keep others who know of his or her history fully informed.

I would also extend this caution to anyone who is battling with emotional illness. Fasting is such a drain on our body and our spirit that we must be very careful if we are already burdened by other significant difficulties.

Because our church runs a therapeutic faith community, a number of persons have come to us with this kind of disorder. We have been able to help many individuals break these cycles and begin to be free. After a period of stability we would support them in trying to fast during one of the church's rotating fasts. But we warn people that this learning journey takes time, so they should satisfy themselves and others that they are in the right place to be able to fast.

If you are addicted to alcohol, drugs (either street drugs or medication), or tobacco, fasting from food will likely be unrealistic. I would caution you against serious fasting until you have resolved these issues, or at least agreed on a way forward under professional supervision. For smokers, in particular, to just stop eating could invoke a whole range of uncomfortable side effects.

Nearly all of us are "addicted" to something, even if it is socially acceptable. The most common compulsion involves caffeine, generally in the form of coffee, tea, soft drinks, or energy drinks. Other addictions include chocolate and other sweets, as well as potato chips and other salty snacks. Even though I know they are poison to me, I have had a compulsive love for dry roasted peanuts. When I eat them (often a whole packet!), my stomach gets upset.

Many of us don't really admit that we are hooked. We tell ourselves that we could do without a cup of coffee if we wanted. We don't realize how dependent we have grown until we stop consuming a certain food or drink for a period of time. Before trying a water-only fast, it is often more helpful to do occasional fasts from these specific foods or beverages in order to break the power of these addictions.

Be prepared for the unexpected, however. You may well start feeling depressed as you experience inverted anger because of having your comfort food taken away. The emotional struggle of depriving oneself of an addiction to food will be a surprising battleground for many. You may find yourself having a temper tantrum. Or you may begin to get headaches and/or dizziness due to the lack of caffeine. It is common for this preparation period to be worse than the early days of an actual fast. The preparation can turn out to be a fast all of its own!

One final word about these problematic compulsions. Though many people are unaware of this, most popular soft drinks contain a number of addictive chemicals. So be sure to stop drinking them before starting a fast, as it will otherwise be a real shock to you when you do.

But let us now assume that you are fully prepared and are into the countdown to begin your fast.

Exploring the Discipline

If you have never done a water-only fast you should probably start with a short fast, say four hours, that involves missing one meal (and perhaps several cups of coffee or tea!). Even for such a brief fast I would encourage you to take into account the guidelines we have already discussed (see Chapter 8). Use your time wisely. Perhaps you can devote an hour or more to intercessory prayer.

After several of these fasts you will probably be ready to commit yourself to eight hours, then to twelve hours, and then to your first twenty-four-hour water-only fast. Here the physical consequences of depriving yourself of food will likely be more noticeable. The way your body reacts to these short fasts will be an indication of how you are going to fare with longer fasts. Be mindful that the process you go through in these first brief fasts could establish your routine for years to come.

A twenty-four-hour fast is the maximum some people can do, while others will recognize that that they are capable of fasting much longer. If you feel, after doing several twenty-four-hour fasts, that you may be able to try something longer, you must be responsible before the Lord, your family, and those supporting you for deciding on what lengths of fast to practice. A three-day water-only fast (or perhaps even less than that) is the most that some people can safely handle because of their health, lifestyle, or commitments. If this applies to you, you shouldn't consider anything more demanding unless the Lord changes your circumstances to make it possible. Many of my examples are drawn from extended fasts of fifteen to thirty days. However, I know of many others who will experience equivalent reactions during fasts of seven days or even three days. For this reason I have resisted the temptation to define the length of an extended fast. This is something that will be uniquely identified during your fasting journey. You will find out how long it takes to reach the end of your own physical resources.

I am operating from the simple assumption that, regardless of the length of your fast, your experiences of extended fasting will be similar to my own. You may find yourself feeling something less extreme than I have. But I would rather be guilty of conveying a more depressing picture than of offering you hope that doesn't materialize!

Choosing When to Fast

Abstaining from food during the winter can be quite difficult since your body has less fuel to generate heat. You will get into bed feeling cold, and it seems to take all night to get warm. And then when you get up in the morning your body chills immediately. Some people find that this affects them even in a twenty-four-hour fast.

During an extended fast your body's immune system doesn't function at 100 percent, so you need to try to keep your body temperature constant in order to avoid catching a cold or the flu. I am thankful I have never had to break a fast for this reason, but I have been aware of the vulnerability of my body during wintertime fasts.

The other catch is that because you have no energy you can't get warm by exercising. My knees, together with the top of my bald head and the back of my neck, seem to suffer most. With our home's central heating system working efficiently I can still feel chilled and uncomfortable, especially my hands, knees, and feet. Even during warm weather, I have worn a coat in the house.

So, if possible, I would recommend doing extended fasts in the warm time of the year. If you feel led to fast during cold weather, however, stay inside as much as you can.

I have always found it best to start a twenty-four-hour fast in the evening. This allows you to break the fast the next evening and therefore to sleep both nights with a relatively full stomach. You will eat, let's say, no later than six o'clock the first evening and then break the fast by eating sometime after six the following evening.

For fasts longer than twenty-four hours, I'd suggest that you eat your last meal in the evening and then break the fast with a light meal in the evening two or more days later. For me, six o'clock in the evening has always been the magic time for starting and stopping a fast. When I have participated in a fasting rotation with others, we have usually found that this was the best transition time from one person's fast to the next. Others prefer different options. What is important is that you have a routine, thereby reducing the stress that accompanies fasting.

Contending with Eating Habits

Overeating before a fast will make getting into the fast that much harder. The instinct to try to hoard food in your stomach will be strong. Please do enjoy your last meal: savor the flavors, sense the saliva glands releasing, enjoy the aromas and tastes. But do not overeat. Binge eating beforehand merely increases the agony, because breaking into the fast is the first battle. Leading up to a fast, eat modest amounts of the kind of foods that digest easily, such as steamed vegetables, soups, broths, fruits, and salad.

Most people have very little idea how much time they actually spend eating and drinking. Because it is such a big part of our lives, we mostly do it automatically without thinking much about it. When we fast we begin to realize that getting a bottle of water or a glass of tap water takes a lot less time than making numerous cups of coffee or going to get a Coke several times a day. And because meals are social occasions for most of us, we don't associate eating with consuming a couple of hours of time each day.

We must be prepared for rebellion. Every hour, especially at mealtime, our body will scream out that we have not eaten. Though it varies from one person to another, most of us will be surprised at the extent of the protest. It will likely be especially bad when you go to bed. I would sometimes try to fool my body by drinking a glass of warm water. It helped a little, but be prepared for a battle. Hold steady.

Fasting with an Open-Ended Commitment

When you start fasting it is always helpful to do it for a fixed period, especially if you are abstaining from food. As you build up to longer fasts through practice, you will learn how to prepare for a fast, how your body and spirit react to a time of fasting, and how to break a fast. As you get more experienced, fasting can become more open-ended.

I have done several fasts with no fixed end in mind. While preparing for one particular fast, I wrote in my journal, "I have been wondering how long this fast should last, and my instinct is to not break it till I have seen the Lord's full provision for the future." My attitude on this occasion was that I was willing to fast close to death, if that was needed. I did not intend to break the fast until I either had the knowledge I needed or was told directly by the Lord that I should stop because I had done enough.

You must not make such commitments, however, unless you have been fasting for some time and know for certain that this is what the Lord is requiring. It is also important that those who have spiritual oversight in your life agree that this is the route to take.

If your schedule permits and your family and supporters approve, you should be able to enter an open-ended fast. Your next battle will be with yourself: whether you will surrender and submit to the Lord and His control, trusting that He will take care of you. At its heart, fasting is a declaration of trust that, although you choose to go into it, you know He will bring you out of it.

If you are beginning an open-ended fast, that means you are planning to fast until the Lord tells you your objectives are achieved. Therefore your goals must be absolutely clear, realistic (with the Lord's help, of course), and capable of being easily measured. Apart from your fasting, you have no power to bring about the fulfillment of your goals. It is critical that others have agreed with your goals. If they just laugh at you, even though they honor and love you, then you can be sure you need to revise them!

The goals must be easily measurable, which means you will clearly know when they are met. Again, talk to those close to you to see what they think; since they are not fasting they can be much more objective about testing this.

Nevertheless, let me caution you about writing clear goals and sticking to them through an illustration in my own life. Deep into an extended fast, the Lord told me that He would give me what I asked for and therefore I could break the fast. I knew the Lord was speaking, but I rebelled and told Him that I would not break the fast until I had the knowledge in my hand. He went silent on me for a couple of days, but then gave me a key to the knowledge that I knew was from Him. He still didn't give me the full knowledge, but I broke the fast because I had the reassurance that I needed.

Breaking a Fast Prematurely

I believe that committing to a fast and then breaking it prematurely is dishonoring to the Lord. You have entered into a battle to stand with

Christ, but then withdrawn. I have likened this faithlessness to the judgment we can bring on ourselves when we take the Eucharist wrongly (1 Corinthians 11:27–32). If this happens during your fast you will need to spend some time asking for the Lord's forgiveness, and receiving His forgiveness and forgiving yourself, before trying again. My view is that it is much better to grow slowly in the discipline than to have too many experiences of such failure.

However, you must be prepared to break the fast at any time if your health is clearly suffering. Don't wait for the goal to be met if your body is enduring more than it should be. For instance, if you begin to suspect you have stomach ulcers or some other pain that is beyond the pain of hunger, there is no wisdom in pushing on and perhaps doing physical damage to your body. Talk to those standing with you, and if they agree, stop and get medical advice.

On one occasion I was moving toward the end of a long fast; but unlike all previous occasions I found myself getting concerned, because after about twenty-five days I started feeling ill. This was unusual, since by this time in a fast I am usually relaxed and well into my stride. I had slowed down enough to accommodate my body, and organs such as my stomach and bowel had given up the fight and settled down.

I was concerned that my body was going into a kind of starvation shock, though I felt I still had a lot of stored fats in my body. Yet I felt that for some strange reason I was not converting them into nourishment. I knew about the process of a person's body using up all these stored fats and then beginning to consume healthy tissue, such as muscle. So I began to monitor how I was feeling even more closely, though not terminating the fasting routine.

When you are deep into an extended fast you cannot just start eating. Then at thirty days I broke the fast, having achieved what I wanted. I held steady in the last few days and the situation did not get worse, though I remained uncomfortable.

In Summary

I have introduced some of the key factors to consider when embarking on water-only fasting. This is a journey I would encourage every Christian to embark upon, while being mindful of the challenges.

I am aware that my experience is not typical. My ministry and calling in Christ have meant that extended fasting has been a necessity. My short, stocky body and slower metabolism pushed me to fasting for thirty or more days, which I recognize would be inadvisable if not impossible for many people. Nonetheless, as you read on I hope that you too will want to take up this discipline in whatever way the Lord enables you.

12.

THE UNIQUE BENEFITS
OF A WATER-ONLY FAST

Water-only fasts are a type of fast unlike any other. One pays a physical cost that does not occur in any other form of fast. But this dimension also brings a complete new set of potential benefits, which we will consider in this chapter. They are not what most people would consider benefits, but from God's perspective and in the Kingdom of God they are pearls of great price.

The length of the fast is not the issue—the sacrifice is. A person on a three-day fast may go through the same intense struggle that another did on a three-week fast. But as the lengths of your fasts increase, the benefits are likely to become more pronounced. God has numerous other ways of bringing you these benefits if you are unable to fast in this way. An extended fast, however, definitely helps soften the ground of your spirit and reshape your emotional life, and it helps you engage the spiritual world.

It is essential that we all acknowledge our uniqueness, not just as male and female but also as individuals. None of us are naturally Christ-like. We all have to discover this—under His instruction, learn from others, and make personal changes in our values, attitudes, and behavior. [1]

We shouldn't enter the Christian life believing that we are now perfect and have no need to do any more. Some seem to presume that salvation is what matters, and once we have it that is the end of the matter. I must say that this is not the case for any of us. We all need further change to become more like Christ.[2]

One of the best ways for us to change in a positive way is to discipline our bodies, as Paul suggested in 1 Corinthians 9:27. This will help us become mellower, flexible, gracious, and honorable in our behavior. This and more will be the outcome of our fasting in a mature way, if we let it.

A Place of Brokenness

Water-only fasting, especially for an extended period, takes you to places within you that are not for the proud. Your vulnerability and weakness caused by fasting should lead to a greater humility, and your surrender to being humbled should lead in turn to brokenness—which is a wonderful benefit for any person.

This is a quiet brokenness that allows you to see life from a different perspective. For some people it is the first time they truly become aware of others. It may result in nearly a trance-like state, in which you see

1   I have written about this in my doctoral thesis, *Becoming More Human: Exploring the Interface of Spirituality, Discipleship and Therapeutic Faith Community* (Bletchley, Milton Keynes, UK: Paternoster, 2005).
2   See P. R. Holmes and S. B. Williams, *Becoming More Like Christ: Introducing a Biblical Contemporary Journey* (Milton Keynes, UK: Paternoster, 2007).

and hear people in a way you had not heard them before. For instance, you notice people rushing around: always under pressure, always in a hurry, always pushing on in life. You note how stressed everyone looks under the pressure of trying to get everything done. You notice how they eat—without thinking about it most of the time. You sit back and watch it all happen. A mere observer, you are no longer part of it. You have, in a sense, opted out for a season. You let this new situation flood you. By fasting you enter a new dimension of yourself, and you get a different view on everything and everyone.

On an extended fast you will likely slow down to a snail's pace. You have to sit most of the time. Even climbing the stairs or walking from the house to the car requires stopping to take a breath. Your heart beats faster than normal with the slightest exertion. You notice the stress your body is under when you attempt the simplest tasks. You may have to pause because you feel dizzy when you stand up. Waking in the mornings, you have to sit on the edge of the bed while you get your balance.

If you are adopting the right spirit toward fasting, you begin to laugh at yourself, noting how arrogantly you have taken for granted the strength in your body and your right to eat and drink whenever you want. Now it has all gone. You have to keep reminding yourself that you are not able to do these things for a season.

You remember eating, and feeling the warm strength of the food in your body giving strength to your muscles. This fuel is no longer yours to enjoy. You may develop a disdain for water. It is sickeningly bland and empty. Yet you have to drink several glasses a day, so you continue to force it down.

You recognize the arrogance of the fast-paced way in which you have lived, pushing everyone around you. You begin to reflect on your lifestyle. You thumb through the pages of your date book and wonder how you did it all.

There have been times when I have sat and cried at the pained void in my stomach, now shrunk to something smaller than my clenched fist. Without food to generate warmth, I have ached with the cold in my body even on warm, sunny days. You also begin to realize how social eating is. I have cried at the loneliness of sitting at the meal table with my family, having just a glass of water in front of me. I have cried at the isolation I have felt—even though nothing has actually changed around me except for the fact that I am not eating.

You are no longer human, like the others around you. You touch upon a brokenness in your life that impacts every part of you, leaving you wanting to lie on the floor, curl up, and sleep—forever.

Your Spirit Takes Authority over Your Body

It is not just your body that feels the denial of food so acutely. You begin to experience a shift in the way you think, in the way that you feel. For instance, sounds are accentuated and smells are sharper. You are more aware. You notice the beauty of things in a way that you have not in the past. You have time to stop and notice, as you don't have the energy to do other things. Even feeding the goldfish seems more important and significant than ever before.

Your body may be in a constant chill. You can sit in the warm summer sun, like our patio looking out over the sea near Dover affords us, but still feel chilled to the bone. Like me, you may be too embarrassed to slip on a winter jacket or ask for a blanket when others are wearing T-shirts.

The cold you sense is your body adjusting to the denial of food. You are choosing to begin a process of slowly dying. But sensing that your spirit is strong, you are continually able to overrule your body's demands. You find your spirit and connect with it in a way that you have not before. You have the time and opportunity to do so now.

You begin to know the difference between your physical body and your intangible spirit. They are two sides of one coin, but for the first time you are seeing the other side more clearly. Your spirit is "you" in a way that your body is not. You know what is meant now by the temporal and the spiritual. Your spirit has the ascendancy over your body, probably for the first time. It is imposing its will on your body. You are giving it no concessions, no morsel of food. It can get used to the idea of having no nourishment, nor any of your attention and time. The continual affirming of this—your spirit over your body—gives you a new sense of your spirit: its will to do, its ability to direct, and its capacity to assert itself.

As I noted in one of my journal entries, this brings a richness of experience to you that you will find no other way. You find yourself as you affirm that your spirit is eternal and what truly matters, whereas your body is temporal, fickle, and vulnerable. Yet one day your body is going to change into something it cannot now be. You now know this is true.

The concept of body-spirit unity comes alive, as you sense you are standing over your body, able to see your physical nature for what it is: self-serving and selfish much of the time. Your body is only part of who you are, not the sum of who you are. You are more than your body, more than your appetites. Yes, you now see that you are much more than your physical drives and appetites. You find *you*.

Without food and sustenance in your body, you are still you. You begin to reflect upon the simple fact that one day your new, glorified body will have no need for food but will be sustained by Christ Himself. You will be free from its pain and limitations as you live without its constraints. You realize that you are touching just a little of this now. But other things are also happening.

Breaking Gluttony

The written testimony of believers following the New Testament period shows that the church at that time had a positive view of fasting as a way of breaking gluttony.[3] Such vision is likely even more needed today. Breaking the habit of eating food is the biggest aspect of the suffering of a fast for most of us: confronting the sheer agony of reaching a mealtime with your body selfishly complaining, with a growling stomach, that it needs food. Instead of giving in, you are telling it to shut up.

Breaking the routine—in reality, the treadmill—of eating is probably one of the greatest needs in the Western world today. Our alarming rate of obesity illustrates this. We eat out of habit, not need; and we eat more than we need, as our weight demonstrates. Our stomachs are so accustomed to getting excess food that they complain when they don't get what they want when they want it. But such gnawings don't mean that we are "starving"; instead, we are merely breaking a routine. I would that everyone could fast for a season just to learn how entrenched and addicted to food we really are!

Breaking the eating addiction—this will be the essence of the battle for most of us. On an extended water-only fast it can take up to eight or even twelve days before your stomach stops growling and gets the message that you are not feeding it. Your stomach finally will submit and go into a sleep-rest state, shrinking to the size of your fist. Your stomach and intestines empty, cleanse themselves, and then rest.

But a range of other things connected with eating happens. Saliva stops secreting in your mouth and the un-stimulated manufacture of digestive acids in your stomach slows down. The pH balance in your body changes as it begins to discharge the stored toxins. As a precaution, if the sensation in your stomach or digestive tract moves from a

---

1   Teresa M. Shaw, *The Burden of the Flesh: Fasting and Sexuality in Early Christianity* (Minneapolis: Fortress Press, 1998), 129–60.

growling hunger pain to a sharp or deep pain, stop your fast and talk to a medical professional.

Other aspects of not eating also surface. You begin to realize how social the routine of eating is for you. Most of us rarely eat alone. Purchasing and enjoying food is typically associated with friendship. We view eating as an experience meant to be shared. When we go on a fast we break much of this contact.

If we are with immediate family, it is important to tell them that we are fasting. It is helpful to sit with our family or friends and drink our water while we watch them feast on savory and sweet foods. I often cook while I am fasting as a way to support Mary and to stay in touch with what is going on. But it is usually better that people outside of your immediate family don't know what you are doing. Therefore you keep away from them at mealtimes. Having said that, though, the contemporary practice of drinking bottled water has added a bit of credibility to the excuse of sitting there, with your spring water in hand, while they eat.

What I am suggesting is that feeling lonely is part of the burden of the fast. Not being able to share meals with people is a big loss. While fasting you are choosing to be isolated, different, no longer one of the gang. By fasting, you are voting yourself out of normal life, out of normal behavior, out of normal friendships. You are choosing a season apart.

Again, I should remind you that the length and even the type of fast is not the key issue. It is what we go through with the Lord in our act of obedience that is critical. One person may be aware that he or she is better able to fast from food than is another. It is important to learn what you are capable and not capable of achieving. Be careful not to assume that everyone is like you. They are not, in many ways.

But something deeper will also be happening in you as you fast, whether for twenty-four hours or twenty-one days, something much more serious than just losing an aspect of our social life upon which we may have come to presume.

Identifying with the Truly Hungry

By going into an extended fast you are, in a sense, taking on a curse of poverty, in a very real way identifying with the sick, poor, and destitute. Most of us have no concept of how prosperous a world we live in until we ourselves are without food. On average, First-World children and adults eat, in calories and nourishment, in one day what a Third-World teenager eats over several days. We consume calorie-enriched foods, high in unhealthy cholesterol, salt, and sugar.

The average North American or European has a remarkable capacity to burn calories, every day eating two to three times the calories of many people in the developing world. We have trained our bodies to eat more than we need. That is why many of us are overweight. But then, when we fast, we are telling our body it is getting nothing. This will be a terrible shock to it.

Although you are reminding your body who is in charge, you are also entering an emotional and spiritual arena that will probably be new territory for you. You begin to find out what it is like to go to bed with an empty stomach. You lie on your bed feeling the ache of your shrinking stomach. While you are trying to sleep, sometimes a hopeless task, you dream of a hot chocolate drink or a snack to help you sleep better. But it is not coming. You are entering the realm that millions around the world live in every day of their lives: poverty, sickness, and hunger.

Having touched this hunger a great deal, I find it hard to view reports of poverty and deprivation on TV or in the press. I frequently travel in East Africa, where daily poverty and hunger is the experience for many. So I am aware more than most what it is like to live with hunger, though traditional fasting will not take you down the road of the bloated, distended stomach of starvation. Nonetheless, you are walking the road with many others—a road you never would have traveled otherwise.

Sleeping is difficult when you are hungry. But another type of poverty also becomes your companion.

You lose weight, especially off your waist, stomach, and backside. You find that you are not comfortable sitting anymore. You are fidgety, restless all the time, as though you are hunting for food. But then you come back to your senses, realizing that you have intentionally separated yourself from food. You are willfully choosing to associate with those who are hungry and poor, those who are separated from the riches and the overabundance of modern Western society. You start to understand God's rage against the manipulative wealth of the rich and His concern for the servitude of the poor. You sit and acknowledge how they feel!

You are voluntarily identifying with the hungry and the poor, at least for a season. In a strange way you sense the approval, even the delight, of the Lord, as you begin to repent for the injustice of the world of which we are all a part.

In Summary

The benefits of water-only fasts, especially extended ones, are life changing. You are tangibly engaging in a new way of looking at your whole life. You discover the reality of the spiritual world, the world that we all live in but ignore so much of the time. You discover what it takes to share deeply in the suffering of Christ and thereby bring more of heaven to earth.

13.

THE PHYSICAL IMPACT
OF AN EXTENDED WATER-ONLY FAST

This chapter will focus specifically on extended water-only fasts, so if you are not considering this type of fast, or are unable to do these fasts, please feel free to skip this chapter. However, you may be interested in my comments regarding the way the human body is designed to cleanse itself during the rigors of water-only fasting. [1]

One of the benefits of abstaining from food is that you learn a lot about your body. Like many people, I would have preferred to have been a bit taller and put on weight less easily. But my body fits me well for the fasting journeys I have taken. I have lots of stored fats, am naturally strong, and have stayed fit for most of my life. Though my

2   Again, I am grateful to general practitioner and nutritionist Brian Mc-Donogh for his assistance in this chapter, though the opinions expressed are my own.

body has served me well, I have had to learn much about it in order to care for it properly.

If you are just beginning to fast, my recommendation—as I have mentioned before—is that you start slowly, all the while talking to close friends or family members about what you are doing. Because all of us are unique and we all have the need to care for our bodies, it is useful to have a sounding board in others to help us monitor what we are experiencing.

So let us understand in a little more detail the physical impact of extended water-only fasting.

Unleashing Free Radicals

When you go on an extended water-only fast unusual things inevitably begin to happen to your body. You put considerable extra strain on the liver, for instance, as it has to process all the toxins being released because you start to digest the fatty tissue that stores some of the toxins in the body. The liver is assaulted by an enormous rush of what are described as "free radicals." You can look at this process during the early part of a fast in one of two ways: either as an attack on the body as these free radicals proliferate, or as a natural cleansing process that you allow your body to go through because it is designed to rid itself of all these toxins in this way. I have always seen it as the latter, a natural process that is healthy for my body in the long run.

Free radicals are supercharged atoms, with an unpaired electron, giving them the capacity to bond. These unpaired electrons link with our own tissue, making them toxic. Antioxidants, on the other hand, offer themselves as "sacrificial lambs" to be attacked and damaged by the free radicals, thus sparing our body's cells. The damaged antioxidants are then passed through the body in the normal way.

Individuals on a water-only fast will not be getting antioxidants through eating, and therefore they will suffer a higher degree of free radical damage if they do not take a precaution. Such a precaution is easily put in place. A water-only fast leeches minerals out of the body, so to avoid free radical damage the water should be filled with minerals. When you fast you cut out all forms of nutrition, but you must somehow allow your antioxidants to work normally. To do this you can take a multivitamin/multi-mineral supplement tablet each day. This is especially beneficial in the early days of the fast when the free radical process is at its most intense.

Taking such a supplement does not add any nourishment or calories to your diet, so you are still maintaining the spirit of the fast. The multivitamin/multi-mineral tablet has no calorie value, but it rewards your body with the needed mineral value. Just one tablet a day will help your body cope.

The Process of Self-Digestion

Most people have accumulated substantial numbers of fat-storing cells (lipocytes). When eating normally, most of us don't burn up all the calories we consume, so our bodies convert some of this extra energy into lipid form and store it in lipocytes. Several days into your fast your body begins to digest fat sources from the most recently created lipocytes.

During the first few days of a water-only fast the body also burns muscle tissue as fuel, converting it into glucose for energy. The body presumes, just like it always has, that it can easily replace this energy later. But as it begins to realize it is not getting such nutrition it moves into survival mode, preserving calories as part of a longer-term survival strategy. In doing so it begins burning stored fats, or ketones, and as ketosis develops the body becomes more toxic because of the release of free radicals and other toxins that are stored in these fats. The body temporarily becomes more acidic with the release and disposal of these free radicals.

The colon also has a tendency to shut down when we are only consuming water, but it is a key player in the detoxification process that occurs as the body digs into its stored fats. Therefore, some have suggested that we should practice herbal-tea-only fasting rather than water-only fasting to help keep the colon functioning. Green tea is most often recommended.[2] I have some reservations about this, however, because green tea contains caffeine. Other herbal teas may be more healthful—for example, red bush tea, which is caffeine-free.

As the fast continues the fats that have been stored longer begin to be absorbed. They are often more toxic and harder to digest, as well as less able to deliver the nourishment the body needs, than the recently stored fats. So the fast gets more difficult, particularly in the second week, when most people's bodies reach fats that have been stored for some time—often for years.

The lipids, or fatty cell membranes, in these cells are not as readily digestible, so extra energy is required to release them and break them down. Among other things, you may experience light-headedness, fatigue, constipation, cold hands and feet, bad breath, skin eruptions, body odor, darker urine, and mucous drainage. We have to make peace with such side effects if we are to support the body cleansing itself in this way.

The process of self-digestion normally proceeds in the following order: First we burn up sugars and then glycogen, or stored sugars. Our body then moves on to fats, skeletal muscle, partial digestion of internal organs, and respiratory and cardiac muscles. This last stage—when the body begins consuming its own skeletal muscle and internal organs—is when we really are starving. The order and timing of this process is precisely coordinated by the brain, with the intent of maintaining the essential organic functions for staying alive as long as possible.

---

1   See Yukihiko Hara, *Green Tea: Health Benefits and Applications* (London: Marcel Dekker, 2005)

Every person's body is programmed in this way. The last tissues to be digested by the body are the muscles responsible for breathing and sustaining the heart. Both of these are essential for maintaining brain function, which is the key physical process for the continuation of life.

Losing Weight

People vary considerably in the way in which they lose weight when fasting. Even with my daily two-mile run/walk, I burn little more than a thousand calories a day, which is below average. In this sense I have a body suited to fasting, as I can last a lot longer! But because of your age, lifestyle, and metabolism you could be one of those individuals who burns three thousand calories or more per day. If so, you will lose weight faster than I do. You need to take these factors into account. Your first extended fast of ten days may be similar to my typical fast of twenty-five days.

On average, most people on a water-only fast will lose about one pound each day. But at the beginning of a fast some folks see weight fall off of them while others lose very little. I know one person who even claimed to put on weight!

On one particular fast I noted no weight loss for four days, but then substantial loss. You might lose as much as twenty pounds in the first ten days, causing your body to reel from the shock. One person might lose ten pounds in three days, while another might only lose three pounds in ten days. Don't expect your body to respond one specific way or like someone else's body has. Instead, make peace with the idea that you are writing some new history with your unique body, tracking new territory, learning new things.

Weight loss will also be determined to some degree by what you ate during the couple of days before the fast, as well as by your metabolic rate—for example, the rate in which your body burns calories. Young people burn significantly more calories than a person like me in his six-ties. Whereas I may burn less than one calorie a minute (the equivalent of one pound of weight per day), a young person could consume two to three times that.

Your lifestyle and activity contribute to your unique metabolic rate. Another factor will be the length of time that you fast. Once the body completes digesting the food in the stomach it will pay attention to the stored fats. Digesting these stored fats is what brings down body weight. Yet another factor regarding metabolic rate is the amount of stored fats that your body has when your fast begins.

Slim people typically don't fare well with extended fasting, as they are usually high metabolic burners and therefore don't store fats the way that people with more sluggish metabolic rates do. If you are slender you likely have less stored fats combined with a faster metabolism, which means that your fasting days are more limited. You will probably reach the "starvation" stage more quickly. Having walked this road with nu-merous people, my observation is that you need to test this yourself by actually fasting. Slim people don't necessarily have less ability to fast, but you may need to accept that you are not one of those who can fast for three or four weeks.

Fasting forces many deep biological changes in our bodies. For instance, there is a change in our bone, muscle, tissue, and fat reserves. If you are one of those people who loses ten pounds in five days you may also begin to lose your physical balance easily. You may not realize it, but the way you walk and carry your body weight—and even the muscle tone and type of muscle in your back, thighs, knees, and calves—has been developed over many years. You have become familiar with this balance and feel. But this can change dramatically as your body loses weight in certain places.

I first lose weight from my backside, then my waist. But I also see reductions in my legs and arms. Others lose weight from their thighs or lower back. You won't realize this until it happens, but losing weight quickly has a real impact on your balance. I have stood up and almost fallen over during fasts, because my normal sense of balance was gone.

Your skeletal and muscular structure can be affected in a number of ways. On one extended fast I had terrible pain in my knees; they felt like they were cracking and snapping. I later saw this as an issue that was being resolved by my obedience, but it was also impacted by weight loss—as my knees are one of the first areas of my body that feel the cold and lack of food, even in the warm sun.

It's helpful to weigh yourself before you begin your fast, recording your weight at the time and then noting changes in your weight every few days. But don't get compulsive about this. I have discovered over the years that during the first few days I will often lose more, or less, weight on one fast than on another. I have not noticed a pattern.

Losing weight is a good thing for most of us. Always remember, however, that this is a side benefit. It should never be a key incentive for fasting to the Lord.

Starvation

When you don't eat, the process of digesting stored fats continues until there are no more readily available lipocytes, or stored fat cells, left in your body. You will notice these stored fats falling off your body in a variety of places. When all these fats are used up, energy will then be sought from more specific protein sources in your body, usually beginning with skeletal muscle tissue.

Technically, it is at this point that the body actually begins to starve. (The next time you announce that you are "starving" after missing one meal, think again!) If you reach this stage in a fast, you could start doing serious damage to your body, and therefore you would need an extremely good reason to keep fasting. Replacing stored fat tissue is easy; you just begin eating again. But restoring depleted muscle is much harder. If it were ever to happen to you, it would be a long-term process requiring professional advice.

If you were to ask people who rested a lot in bed during their fast how long it took them to build up their strength again, they would normally tell you it took the same length of time that they fasted. But when you enter this starvation cycle your body is beginning to damage itself, so recovery is much longer and harder.

This is probably why Matthew 4:2 says that after forty days of fasting Jesus was "starving" (extreme hunger)[3]. After forty days of fasting Jesus had reached the end of His body's natural reserves. If we assume that Jesus was not miraculously sustained, He fasted forty days before His body began to digest vital body tissue. This timeframe would be consistent with a full-framed, healthy, well-nourished person.

So fasting for health purposes is beneficial to a degree, but continuing on when you really are starving is never recommended.

Fasting and the Female Body

Although I have had many conversations with women on the subject of fasting, my experiences obviously come from a male perspective. So to conclude this chapter Susan Williams will share from a personal perspective about some of the unique physical impacts of fasting upon a woman's body.

Peter's experience of fasting is a challenge to us all, but I suspect, particularly to women. I have found my own experience to be typical of many. Even the decision to fast stirs up an emotional reaction disproportionate with the imminent self-denial. I feel a

---

2   Although the NIV text and other translations use the word hungry, the Greek text (*epeinasen*) suggests extreme hunger, 'that he hungered'.

wave of barrenness overwhelm me, like a cold shudder through my spirit.

This should not be a surprise. Many women are sensitive to issues of life and death; so the emotional response to the suffering of a fast can be quite pronounced, even if this is a non-food fast.

Water-only fasts add additional demands. I have to be careful to know when in my menstrual cycle I am fasting and the impact of the loss of nourishment on my body. It is part of taking responsibility for my fast that I avoid, when possible, fasting at a time that will be unhealthy for me.

Like many women, I have a smaller frame than most men. So a twenty-four-hour, water-only fast has a proportionately greater impact. A physically demanding day makes fasting even more of a challenge. My observation is that I experience after twenty-four hours many of the symptoms that Peter describes on the fourth or fifth day of a fast. My metabolism is much faster.

In my daily routine I love tea (with sugar) and I know many women who are also regular snackers or consume frequent small meals rather than the traditional three square meals. Such habits make it even harder to fast, since our bodies are accustomed to the continual supply of nourishment or sugar and caffeine.

When women are pregnant or breast-feeding there are additional complications with fasting. Likewise during menopause or with HRT, fasting may affect the body in unhealthy ways. Talk to a sympathetic doctor. It may be necessary to consider other types of fast, but let's not give up the significance of water-only fasts too easily.

Susan Williams

14.

SURVIVING A WATER-ONLY FAST

The same guidelines should be followed during a water-only fast as with any other fast. In an ideal world, you would have a more relaxed schedule for an extended fast because of its physical demands. When I do an extended fast, however, I generally keep as normal a schedule as possible.

Having said that, it is important to keep in mind the variations from one person to another when it comes to how we react to water-only fasting. If you are only abstaining from one meal, then you obviously don't need to make the rigorous preparations of an extended fast. My focus here is on our attitude toward establishing good routines.

Water, Water, Water!

On the first day or so of an extended fast I usually add a little pure lemon juice to the water as an aid in cleansing my stomach and restoring its pH balance. This, in turn, can also help with sleep in the early days of a fast. The fructose (natural sugar) levels in lemon juice are normally very low. I have a strong conviction that you must not add anything to the water that could be interpreted as nourishing to your body. Any such nourishment could be a compromise to the fast, weakening your resolve and leaving you feeling accused by the Enemy.

When I started fasting in the 1960s tap water was the only option. Perrier wasn't even yet available. But today there is a whole science of water and a plethora of choices. I am sure you will be able to find one that suits you. In my opinion you must not use any of the fortified waters, as their additives could arguably be considered nourishing.

My suggestion is to use tap water or one of the spring waters or mineral waters. Research indicates that the better quality bottled waters are healthier, but please don't spend a fortune on them—especially if you are fasting for provision! Staying with what your body is used to is a good principle. Don't forget the multivitamins with minerals, which are best taken with ample water.

One way to vary the water theme is to drink it hot, cold, or somewhere in between. You will find it much easier to drink hot water in the winter and even warm water in the summer if you feel the chills. Our refrigerator dispenses ice and cold water, which is nice. You can also buy an electric kettle that first filters and then heats tap water. Warm water can be a nice change for a while, until you realize the trick you are playing on yourself.

After a while you are likely to develop a hatred for water, though you must continue to drink substantial amounts of it.[1] You may even get to where you despise the smell of water. You could go for a whole day without drinking any of it. You just want to stop. But your kidneys

---

3   On the other hand, I do need to warn you that drinking an extreme amount of water can result in water intoxication, which can be fatal.

will complain if you do. If I don't drink enough water, I also find that I develop lower back pain and my hands and feet get particularly cold. Being cold makes cold water uninviting, so it is all too easy just to stop drinking water altogether.

The less you drink, the less you want to drink. But the breaking down of stored fats (lipolysis) requires a lot of water. Keep drinking, even though it may be the last thing you want to do.

The Pain Barrier

Some people sail through the early period of a fast and wonder what all the fuss was about. Others are like me—feeling the increasing ache in my body, I rest and go to bed early when I can.

Hunger is just one aspect of the pain barrier that you will need to go through. For many the pain begins with a headache. If you haven't prepared properly, for the first twenty-four hours the pain may take the form of caffeine withdrawal. Into the second and third day there will be a lot more going on. Paradoxically, as your body weakens you will have periods when you feel good in your spirit. The obedience and the declarations you are making by fasting will strengthen you in these early days. At last you are now doing a real fast!

For most of us, the real battle commences after the third day or so. Who is going to win—your stomach or your spirit? Your body or your will? As your stomach empties and your body is forced to begin eating stored fats, you will feel the gnawing hunger in your stomach. The battle will likely get tough.

Most people with normal body weight and metabolism get through the pain barrier between the ninth and the twelfth day. It will likely be that long before you break through into a space of calm hunger. You will have won that round. Now you can settle down for the bigger battles ahead. Pain is a result your body breaking the habit of the intake of food, the routine of always having food in your stomach.

The Problem of Sleep

Normally I am asleep within a minute or two of laying my head on my pillow, although I do have a routine I go through—settling the day with the Lord, sorting all the debris—before I try to sleep. But when I am fasting it will typically take over an hour for me to go to sleep; and then I often wake up at four o'clock. My body tends to go through only one sleep cycle. I can never sleep a full night during an extended fast.

I am not sure why this is, but it seems to be the way for me. I just lie in bed, my stomach aching and my body feeling cold. I can't seem to get enough warmth in my body to be comfortable. You don't realize how important having an adequate body temperature is for sleeping until you can no longer achieve it.

While everyone else is asleep with a full stomach, you may be lying in bed absorbed, even obsessed, by your hunger. You lie there thinking of the tastes that you most enjoy. You may find yourself declaring that you are going to break the fast the very next minute. Or you may fantasize about taking your wife out for an exquisite dinner after your fast. The only relief will be a hot bath. So enjoy the sleep of the first couple of nights during a fast, because as the days go by you will probably need to drink a large mug of hot water before going to bed in order to fool your body into thinking it is getting something!

I don't want to sound too spiritual, but if I can't sleep I will often get up and pray, read Scripture, write in my journal, do some research, or work on a book project. You will find time to do things that you would normally never dream of being able to do. Ask the Lord what book He would have you read. I have read some of the Christian classics that I had not looked at since my youth. I discovered Thomas Merton during one of my fasts, and the writings of the Cappadocian Fathers (fourth-century theologians) on another. Make the time count, as your life at that moment is your intercession. Don't become obsessed by the need to sleep.

Forced to Slow Down

Going on an extended water-only fast should force us to adopt a calmer lifestyle. For me this has been one of the greatest benefits of fasting. None of us has any conception of how fast a pace we maintain until we are forced to stop. Once we begin fasting we quickly learn how much we need to slow down, because of how weak we really are.

As I have previously mentioned, during a prolonged fast I don't even have the strength in my arms to carry my briefcase. I will often need to get someone else to carry things for me, which is humiliating. Sometimes I put things in a plastic bag so they are lighter. And I cannot wear boots or heavy clothing. Heavy shoes are like lead weight.

Our bodies work very hard to provide the energy we need to live. When I do my regular daily exercise I sense by body bouncing back in minutes. But not when I am fasting. I have to abandon my exercise routine since I have no reserves whatsoever. I will have to stop halfway up a flight of stairs and sit down to avoid passing out. Doing the simplest job, like carrying a basket of laundry or cleaning the windows of the car, is a strain. Things like washing the car are out of the question. You have to slow down, limiting your schedule to what is essential, letting go of many of your expectations.

During a fast I would spend entire days just sitting in my chair at home, reading and writing, if I could. Fasting breaks the treadmill, decimates the work drive. Many days I will go into work drinking only water and will not leave my chair the whole morning. It can be a real battle to pretend you are normal—one of the gang—while accepting the constraints of fasting. One has to adopt a quieter lifestyle.

The most important thing to do while you are fasting is to rest. If you are working, come home after work and lie down for an hour. Let your body restore itself as much as it can. Let your spirit also be restored through spiritual disciplines such as reading Scripture or Christian books and meditation. Be aware that your body is not able to bounce back like it normally would. You will be unable to do all the things that you usually do, so honor your body by resting it, by letting it recover as much as it can.

The Scourge of Bad Breath

One of the unexpected and unpleasant side effects of fasting for more than a few days is bad breath.

The saliva in your mouth performs several functions. One of its key roles is to carry and distribute antibodies that kill unwelcome bacteria in the mouth, thus keeping the mouth fresh. Saliva also lubricates the mouth, gums, and teeth, helping to avoid bleeding and disease in the mouth and gums. When you stop eating, your salivary glands go to sleep. Since you aren't chewing food, they aren't needed; you are no longer stimulating them. Consequently, your mouth begins to feel like sandpaper. Because no new saliva is being secreted, your mouth also begins to turn into a septic tank. After three or four days this process becomes irreversible.

The smell is mostly the result of the breaking down of all the microbial food deposits that are left in your mouth from your last few meals. Brushing your teeth doesn't remove them all. So during the fast this process gets worse.

Fortunately—or maybe unfortunately—you won't notice the smell yourself. But everyone around you will. I have gone to parties where I could consume only water but also had to avoid people due to the odor coming from my mouth. Warn those closest to you that this is going to happen. I noted in one of my journals on day six of an extended fast,

"Yesterday was the first real bad breath day. I apologized to the family, but they were polite and said they did not notice."

You might vow to brush your teeth every hour, but it won't work. Within a few minutes the smell returns. You might try mouthwash; but again the smell returns. You could put a small menthol crystal in the water you are drinking, which may help a little. But don't put the crystals directly in your mouth, because they will burn a hole in your tongue!

Some people suck on peppermint candy as an attempted remedy. But if you are prone to acid reflux, peppermint can make the problem worse. Gastroesophageal reflux, as it is called, is caused by a weakening of the valve between the esophagus and the stomach, resulting in foul gases escaping from the stomach into the mouth. Beware that mints can affect the one-way valve and exacerbate the reflux. Out of concern for others I have resorted to sucking mints, though I find that this only works for five or ten minutes—and I have had to accept the fact that I am taking some mint into my stomach.

Find out what is best for you, but avoid mints with sugar or sucrose. I use dental floss regularly and brush my teeth at least twice a day. Over the years I have tried all kinds of things to help my bad breath, but nothing has really worked. And after you break the fast it will still take a couple of days to get back to a healthy state. So if you are around other people you may need to continue doing something about your bad breath.

Note that the changes in your body caused by fasting may also lead to mild toothache, mouth ulcers (canker sores), or bleeding of the gums. Don't panic if your gums begin to bleed—just rinse out your mouth. My lips will often begin to crack and bleed, probably due to the lack of saliva in my mouth. I constantly want to lick them, but my mouth is dry. Because of the lack of salivation you may also discover, like I have, that you develop a slight sore throat that will come and go.

Other Side Effects

A number of other unexpected things may begin to happen to your body. My eyes tire more quickly during an extended fast, and my eyes water—sometimes badly. Oftentimes I can't read for more than half an hour before I have to close my tired eyes for a few minutes. On one fast my eyes tired more as the fast continued.

My nasal passages tend to dry up during a prolonged fast. As toxins are released, something like sties may appear around your eyes or on other parts of your body. As just mentioned, ulcers may appear in your mouth as the saliva dries up. In a real sense, these are actually good things: evidence of the breaking down of the fats and toxins stored in your body.

Other annoying side effects may include unexpected flatulence, feeling like you need to have a bowel movement when there is nothing to move, and having really dark urine despite the fact that you are drinking lots of water. As already noted, you may have trouble sleeping. During the day you may be restless. Unable to sit still for long, you may feel compelled to get up and move around, yet you have little energy when you do. Restlessness can consume you.

Likewise, the waves of hunger can be relentless. I crave the silliest of foods: for example, potato chips (which I normally don't eat), sardines, salami, and cream cake. I have found myself dreaming up the craziest of meals, vowing to cook them when I get off the fast. (I never do.) Some of this imagining is fuelled by television, where everything is centered around food. I find I especially have a craving for salty snacks, probably because salt is one of the first things that your body runs out of, particularly in hot weather when you are sweating a lot.

On the hand, however, there are some positive side effects of extended fasts. After a week or so your body will begin to benefit from the release of toxins. This will often first show in your skin, as it becomes clearer. I have noticed that my senses become much more acute, especially my hearing and sense of smell. I seem to have more connectedness with the material world. Nature begins to sing to me. Perhaps the "death" happening within me enhances my appreciation for life.

It isn't uncommon for people who don't even know I am fasting to say that I look contented and relaxed, though this may not be how I'm feeling on the inside. Even the dark lines around my eyes go unnoticed. And after breaking a fast I frequently become aware that I had greater intellectual and spiritual clarity during the fast. Issues sometimes become clearer. But at the time you aren't always aware that this is the case, because all you sense is the gnawing in your stomach.

In Summary

Completing a fast of any length is a huge achievement, and you should be righteously proud of doing so. When it is over, share with others, without boasting, some of the journey. Give yourself time to reflect on the experience and on what you have learned about yourself, your body, and your addictions to food. The benefits are numerous if you are willing to appropriate them.

Along with this, enjoy the simple joy of eating again: being with your family and friends and having the companionship of your favorite foods. Buying a good cut of meat or fresh fish and cooking up a treat for yourself and your friends can be a very meaningful celebration. (Just don't do it immediately after a fast!)

THE EMOTIONAL FALL-OUT

If you are not accustomed to fasting, even the shortest fast can produce a range of responses. As you become more experienced, however, it is more likely that many of these responses will arise only after the first few days. The overall impact on your body will be positive and healthy, though at the time you don't feel it because of the misery you are experiencing. Your body will benefit all the while that your will and spirit take authority over your body.

On more than one occasion I have found myself moving from the initial physical pain of the lack of food to a much more profound emotional pain for what I might be carrying from the recent past. Maybe some hard words were spoken to me or I have feelings of being abused by someone, which I had not really owned. Grieving the loss of your emotional attachment to food may well transition to emotional pain in areas of your life that need some attention. I have been surprised at how the Lord cleverly links together these dynamics when we are weak, available, and more vulnerable to Him. Fasting can be a time of emotional cleansing.

The Plague of Irritability

Because you will probably be quite difficult to live with during an extended fast and while breaking the fast, you need to get the blessing of your spouse or roommate/roommates beforehand. I get very short-tempered and feel on a short fuse most of the time. I am sure you also will be prone to bouts of anger and irritability. So make peace with yourself, your spouse, and others close to you before you begin. You will need their support.

I have known people who missed one meal while working with me or standing with me in leadership, and you would think from their level of irritability that they were on a forty-day fast! On the other hand, a friend of mine doing a seven-day fast was as mellow as they come. Be prepared for any outcome when you and others are fasting, and be especially vigilant with those—including yourself—who enter the commitment rather casually and then suddenly begin to go through mood changes.

During an extended fast you won't have the resources to maintain your ordinary routine. You won't be able to carry your normal load, and neither will you be able to be your normal self. You need to make peace with this, and those close to you need to understand this. The key for me has been to go to work as usual, so that other people's lives are disrupted as little as possible, but then to give myself some slack with the pace of the day and the intensity of my normal schedule.

Having nothing in your stomach will deeply impact your temperament. You probably will be a bear, showing none of the mellowness you would normally display. Eating has a way of soothing both the body and the soul. You are being denied this comfort. So you will feel like a child who is punished by getting no sweets or a teenage who is told "No."

It's frustrating to feel like you're being punished. Yes, you know you are doing this for the Lord. Yes, you knew it would hurt. You knew it would be difficult. But secretly you hoped you would cope better. When the reality hits that the only thing you can swallow is water, you will be annoyed with yourself and everyone else. I would bite people's heads off for the most trivial reasons. I would get annoyed when things didn't go my way. Beware, and make sure those close to you are aware.

Some people panic at the thought of missing a meal and therefore do not take well to fasting. If you are one of those people, then please enter this arena carefully. I have seen people change in quite negative ways just because they denied themselves coffee. You would have thought they had a major mood disorder. Don't assume that everyone will react the same; the length and the type of abstinence is not the guide of how people will behave.

The Fear Factor

People also vary in the degree to which they are controlled by fear. When you feel hunger pains in your stomach, you may panic and think you have stomach ulcers. Or you may be afraid that you can't make it for a whole day without food, in which case you may need to reassess your ability to abstain. Perhaps you experienced hunger or poverty in your childhood; that could certainly create additional challenges for your fast.

Fear is part of the cocktail of feeling that will surface during the early part of a fast, especially your first extended fast. Like all emotion, fear can be either good or bad, either an ally or an enemy. But in some ways fear is a unique emotion, since it is wired into the body. There is a growing consensus that our nervous systems mediate a fundamental form of unconditional fear.[1]

---

1   J. Panksepp and J. B. Panksepp, "The Seven Sins of Evolutionary Psychology," *Evolution and Cognition* 6, no. 2 (2000): 108–13.

As far as we know, fear is the only emotion that is neurologically woven into the fabric of our bodies. It needs to be, because we all need the "fight or flight" emotion to guarantee we are able to respond quickly and make the right choices when danger or threats appear. But that is not really the kind of fear I am talking about. This, rather, is an emotional foreboding, like a fear of hurting your body. This is the fear of denying your body food, the fear of not being able to eat.

The fear of doing a fast can be forbidding and frightening, even overwhelming. Your body will do things it has never done before. You are entering new territory—outside the comfort zones of food, drink, and self-pleasure. Your body will complain in all kinds of eloquent ways.

Somewhat irrationally, fear at times will give way to panic, which then gives way to feelings of disobedience when you break a fast because of the fear. Be prepared for these deep inner emotional conflicts. They come as a result of your feelings and belief that you are making yourself sick, that you are doing damage to your body. Your mind plays tricks on you, and so do your fears and imagination. But on the other hand, as you begin to connect with your fears you may feel accusations that you are indulging yourself—focusing on yourself rather than the Lord. The fear factor will arise at some time for the majority of us, gnawing away at our confidence and resolve. Hold steady; you will get through it.

Another related issue can be the memory of previous fasts. Fasting can get harder if past fasts have been tough or complicated. Here's a quote from my journal in regard to a fast I did in 1994: "I guess it is because I have fasted so often before that this time even the decision to go on a fast is causing shock waves in my body. Almost the moment I committed to this fast for the Lord I began to feel like I know I will in a week. Body cold, hunger, heavy head, fragile, and all else." At the end of the first day of the fast I wrote, "I'm so very uncomfortable, very cold, restless, uneasy. Need to have a hot bath and go to bed. God help me." This fast turned into a twenty-five-day fast and was a defining experience in my life.

You can try to let go of any trauma associated with previous fasts; but your body remembers what you put it through, and those memories will quickly return as you enter into another fast. So each fast can get harder. The minute now that I commit to a fast, and engage the memories, I feel waves of nausea.

I am suspecting that my days of extended fasting may be over. I am well, and fasting has not done me any long-term harm. In fact, the discipline and healthful aspects of fasting have been formative in who I am. At times, even now, when I fill a glass with water the memory of all the pain floods back. Although I now enjoy drinking tap water, I lived with this trauma for many years.

There comes a point when some of us are no longer called to fast. I have begun to experience this in recent years. Interestingly enough, this also coincided with a season of harvest in my ministry, with a wave of books and anointing that I sense is drawing on a substantial spiritual bank account from my decades of fasting. Having said that, I don't see that my fasting days are completely over. I am doing a partial fast as I write this book.

Your Vulnerability

Allow me to quote from my journal again: "I am continually irritable, sensing a loss of temper. I realize I am on a short fuse. I want to go to bed at seven or eight in the evening, but when I am in bed all I feel is the ache in my body. You realize that being busy all day helps, because at night you just lie there and feel the pain. It's an emotional roller coaster."

Some people only need to stop eating for one meal before they get heavily into self-pity, remorse, and even panic. If you fit into this category you may want to find a non-food type of fast. And if you are going to react badly to sitting at the table but not eating, then stay away! Don't allow your baggage to hurt others.

You will likely develop an irrational jealousy of people who are living a normal life that includes eating. You know this is irrational, because you have chosen to do this. But you still feel angry that others are not going through the pain you are. Conversely, you may feel contempt for others because they need to depend on food. This inverted pride is fed in part by the emotional roller coaster you are riding.

I find that I am particularly vulnerable emotionally to attacks from others while I am fasting. You may not realize how fragile you are until someone tells you off or threatens you with strong words. You are easily shaken and upset. You don't have the resilience or strength to hold firm. This is another emotional roller coaster.

You will probably have a total lack of energy. I have to prepare myself to waste time (by my standards) for short stretches by just sitting and reading or flicking through the TV channels. After four or five days I begin to find some peace in committing myself to the long haul of an extended fast. I even have bursts of energy.

Some people experience intellectual sharpness and clarity of thought while on a fast. Others find it very difficult to concentrate and feel semi-moronic. What one experiences on a fast in this regard will be determined by a complex range of factors, including body mass and weight, circumstances at home and work, care in preparing for the fast, lifestyle during the fast, and much more. Some will feel a need for comfort and intimacy. Others will experience a permanent dull ache, able to think of nothing but their hunger. What becomes evident is that the Lord will be taking you down a path unique to you. Surrender to it: settle down and enjoy the moment of obedience to Him.

I have to confess that I fall into the category of those who are consumed by hunger and rarely notice much else. I have a work colleague who knows when I am fasting and does not allow me to make any important decisions. I treat the time when I am fasting as though I am going through permanent jet lag—a time when I feel OK but need to be aware that I have lost perspective. The hunger can be all consuming.

I often feel a lethargic indifference to anything and everything. "You sort it out" often becomes my mantra. I find it more difficult to carry responsibility for my business when I am fasting. I need to delegate more. I can't get my mind around the issues as easily.

I will often adopt the mindset that I will do what I am told, though much of the time, truthfully, I couldn't care less. I am consumed by the feeling of the dying inside of me. Despairing depression comes in waves. I feel sorry for myself, for what I have done to myself. I just sit and mope. After the first few turbulent days the body settles down.

Adjusting in Your Spirit

The response in the core of your being to this new situation should be to seek the strengthening of your spirit and resolve as the days go on. The big battle will take place in the first few days. If you are able to gather strength in your spirit in these early days then you will do well. If you become consumed with the hunger, depression, and darkness of the fast, you may be tempted to cave in and break the fast.

If you are new to fasting, don't be surprised if the spiritual onslaught of the darkness of the fast occurs within hours of beginning a fast—or before you even begin. This often catches people by surprise. You have made a significant declaration, a decision to deprive yourself of something that gives you life. As soon as this takes place you are quite likely to feel the difference. It is a time of adjustment to the denial you chose.

You also symbolize and relive in some ways dying in your own life. Put bluntly, water-only fasting is a barbaric practice, a slow killing of oneself by voluntary surrender and choice. Sounds extreme, doesn't it? That's because it is! It separates you from others, as you are not eating. You are different, not able to join in with others or with life.

The longer you fast, the more darkness you may sense. Having said that, though, the length is not nearly as important as your heart obedience and its effect on you. You need to prepare yourself for the impact the fast will have on you. How much darkness will you experience, and how quickly? And in what spirit are you going to enter into the fast? People are often surprised how quickly the spiritual awareness of the reality of the fast hits them, before they have missed even one or two meals.

During the first week of one of the longest fasts I ever did, my wife and I had a deep personal shock: our home was broken into. I wrote in my journal at the time: "Mary called to say that our house had been broken into. They broke two front doors, stole all Mary's jewelry, Indonesian ivory box, twelve collectible plates, and lots of other things, including a valuable Wedgwood jar. Came home to the police and Mary in shock and tears. All very exhausting. Spent the evening repairing the doors and putting new locks on them." The shock of this was temptation enough, for a moment, to break the fast. But instead the break-in strengthened my resolve to continue.

Feeling Oppressed

The oppression of the fast in the first few days will likely be in part because of others adjusting, conveniently forgetting what you are doing and demanding that you be normal. This is especially true if you have young children. They will not understand your not eating. In addition, the purpose of the fast will be questioned by the Enemy. He will interrogate every resolve you have made, not wanting you to hold steady. I have experienced avalanches of problems in the early days of a fast: money problems, hassles with children, power struggles, relational conflicts, and the Enemy gnawing away at my personal weaknesses. Be prepared!

I sometimes sense a demonic mocking, alongside a sense of accusation about the stupidity of what I am doing. I am tempted to see God as a tyrant to require this of me—forcing me to do this, beating me into weak submission before being nice to me again. I have passing thoughts that He is malevolent and unreasonable, a taskmaster who takes but does not give.

But then I have to say that I am sorry, realizing that I fear Him in a righteous way and am choosing to do this for myself as well as for Him. As I recorded in my journal one time, "This fast is of my freewill, and I give my weakened and frail condition to Him as a free offering. My weak, fragile self is all I have to give at the moment. If He can delight in this, then He is indeed a remarkable God."

I have constant feelings of spiritual barrenness. You may be one of the fortunate ones God talks to during a fast, but most of the time I don't hear Him nearly as clearly as when I am not fasting. You get used to the barrenness, however, in anticipation of the time when you break the fast and the Lord begins to talk to you again. You somehow know this, but it doesn't necessarily help in the dark days of the fast.

One time I was bombarded on the twenty-first day of a fast with thoughts of breaking the fast. Let my diary tell you what happened: "Every few minutes thinking of food and drink. Found myself frequently going to the fridge to get some juice or nibbles. Have not had such a barrage of temptation for a long time. Here I was thinking that I was now cruising; yet I find myself really being barraged by masses of clever ideas for breaking the fast. . . . How my body aches for the sun and food. . . . I will need a lot of grace and Holy Spirit support to make it through this day."

But for some of us the biggest problem will be the relational issues.

Relational Issues

It is very important that you have someone walk alongside you in your fast. Don't choose someone close to you who is angry with you because you are doing the fast. An extended fast will impact everyone else around you, whether or not they know you are fasting. You cannot hide from people's spirits what you are choosing to do. The deprivation you are requiring of your body will be sensed by others, so assume they will notice it—even if only indirectly.

At times you will need to talk to someone who brings an objectivity that you lack, someone you can talk to about what is happening to you. You don't have to be a hero or a solitary saint. That attitude just adds to the burden. You need someone to talk to, ideally comparing notes with fasts that person has done.

The individual you talk with will need to be able to cope with the spiritual pressure and honest despair that you go through. So don't look for someone who is vulnerable, such as a young Christian. Enjoy sharing the journey with them.

Let me end this chapter with some comments from my wife, Mary, who has always stood by me in these sometimes-tough times. Here are some of her thoughts and observations:

> When Peter and I were married almost thirty-five years ago, his understanding of the outworking of marriage was that the most important thing each of us could bring to the marriage was to maintain our personal walk with the Lord. He always interpreted this as a personal responsibility. However, when Peter fasted, especially the water-only extended fasts, this line blurred and became very cloudy. I would wake up most mornings feeling trapped in the same closet with him, unable to escape from what he was doing even if I wanted to. I needed to be patient with him, while portraying "business as usual" to the outside world and to our young son, who did not understand the dynamics at times, with me eating but Daddy not.

I believe God is amazingly creative, as seen in nature, as well as a God of balance, as also seen in nature: one God in a relational Trinity, living both inside and outside "the box." God sees our world and yet has a perspective that is much bigger than ours. He does not stay in our "box," but is also outside of it. This is the way Peter and I have sometimes been asked to live—taking separate journeys but simultaneously standing together.

Hiding what Peter was really doing, without being deceptive, was particularly difficult. Peter would remind me that life goes on, business goes on, and even children go on. But how could I go on with normal living while I knew he was "dying." I was being required to live in the spiritual world while walking in the physical world. Some would see or sense that business *wasn't* as usual, so it felt like I was always living in no-man's land.

Peter is the only person I have known who has had the capacity and calling to go on water-only fasts of almost forty days. I, on the other hand, struggle—and I mean struggle—with missing even one meal! Having a metabolism that requires small amounts of food at frequent intervals, I discovered shortly after we got married that this difference was just another way in which God put together two people who came from diametrically opposite corners of life. Fortunately we have a big God, and both of us have big hearts. As I get older I can see this as God's opportunity to balance us out . . . on a good day, that is!

Another facet of fasting is how it both exposed and changed my perspective. I suppose I had always confused "Christ-likeness" and "doing great feats for God" with perfection. So my first shock was that people have the capacity to fast not in isolation but in a family context, even though we are not always the easiest people to live with! And as with most nuclear families, when one suffers we all suffer.

So the truth is that Peter's fasting has been very hard work for us all. In today's 24/7 world, life goes on despite his stopping to fast. But at times it is good to stop—to get off the high-speed train and slow down. We don't have built in to our lives the accommodating of such spiritual disciplines. We've lost it to our peril, I am afraid to say.

Another surprise to me was the impact of fasting on our marriage. When Peter engaged the reality of both the spiritual world and his own personal pain, I can only say it was like consistently waking up in the morning and finding yourself on the frontline in your nightclothes!

As to whether Peter consulted with me before a fast: yes, he would always show me his date book, identifying the only windows where it would be feasible. The good news was that when he was fasting for provision or a breakthrough I could always witness with the need for desperate measures, because the situation was getting serious.

The hardest thing about the timing of Peter's fasts was the simple reality that there was never, from a woman's perspective, a good time to fast! Suffice it to say, any fast was always a day too long! And, as Peter often says, it was a time of vulnerability and a time of God not talking to him. But the Lord would often talk to me during those times, which was sometimes confusing to one or both of us!

Overall, I believe "disorientating" would be the best word to describe my feelings on the subject. Fasting has facilitated touching both the highs and lows of my own walk with God. God did meet me in amazing ways during Peter's fasts, especially the extended ones. But somehow He always had a way of meeting me and speaking to me from the opposite direction, as men and women, in general, and Peter and I, in particular, are so different.

Another shock was that Peter's fasting would sometimes give me a sense of rejection. The implication was that I had no part in what he was doing. It could even feel like waking up and finding you are married to a stranger. So I would say, from a wife's relational perspective, that Peter's fasting has always included a sense of redundancy and/or rejection. Food is one of a man's basic needs, and all the affirming ways of providing it for him have to be given up. When Peter stopped eating there was nothing I could do but sit, watch, wait, and persevere—with the "business as usual" sign up.

The steps I take to prepare myself for an extended fast are threefold:

1. I batten down the hatches, preparing for the emotional/ spiritual roller coaster.
2. I remind myself that nothing is as it appears to be: it is like living between "the end of the beginning" and "the beginning of the end."
3. The sum of the first two make it essential for me to make provision to get away emotionally from the intensity of it all, while needing to be kind to myself by not trying so hard to "get it right." It's like an intense time of spring cleaning: every woman knows that is a time when things have to get worse to get better, because everything must first be moved. But women tend to do this cleaning in "relationship," and by its very nature fasting feels far more like doing it all by yourself in isolation.

The "Daniel fast" is an interesting idea, as it becomes a way of life. I also believe that Daniel was a single man! The best way I can describe handling this is by taking it one day at a time. It is always much easier if you do not have to cater to a large family at the same time that your husband is on the Daniel fast. Cook for the whole family as healthy as you can. Then call a friend when you need space and a treat!

Hopefully, over the years I have made peace with the fact that fasting is one of the spiritual disciplines, and a *gift* as well. Since none of us have all the gifts all the time, I have spent our marriage finding the discipline of complimenting Peter, instead of trying to keep up with him.

Mary M. Holmes

HOW TO BREAK A WATER-ONLY FAST

The importance of being careful in breaking a water-only fast cannot be emphasized enough. Once your body has gone through the shock of breaking the food habit and has conceded defeat and settled down, it is important that you wake it slowly. Gently does it. Even on a relatively short fast of, say, twelve hours, you shouldn't just sit down and eat a normal meal. You should build up to full eating over a twenty-four-hour period. The general rule for a shorter fast is that it takes the same amount of time to break the fast as the length of the fast itself. After an extended fast, I have found that I need to allow up to eight days to break the fast.

I need to make an important comment here. It will take far more discipline for you to break the fast in a responsible way than it ever took for you to abstain from food. Not eating is absolute, but when you begin to eat you will have the whole world of food before you. Breaking a fast has few rules, so you have to write some of your own as you wake your body from its slumbers.

As mentioned previously, breaking even a short fast should be done with much care. Don't dismiss its significance. Abstaining from just one meal can be an emotional experience and have a backlash. Be careful not to say silly things like "I will never do that again"—because the Lord may ask you to! And after you eat again, notice that you may be particularly hyper with the food in your stomach. Be careful to read the rest of this chapter as background, even though you may not be engaging in longer fasts yet. The understanding will be helpful for you.

At the other end of the fasting spectrum is an open-ended fast. Here the decision to break the fast is a significant one and must be done with care. Write out a list of reasons why you feel it is right to break the fast. Think this through very carefully, being brutally honest about what you are thinking. Are you being pressured? Is this the right time? Don't rush your decision.

Talk to the person who is walking with you in your fasting journey. Write down the reasons why God and that person are able to confirm that you have achieved what you set out to do. Record how this witnesses to you. It is very easy in your weakened state to break a fast, but do not make the decision in a knee-jerk way.

I normally look in three areas for confirmation. First, I have done, or the Lord has done, what I set out as the goal before I began: there is some evidence that it has been achieved. Second, my mentor is in agreement that this is the case. Third, emotionally I feel the duty lifting that led me to fast in the first place. If at least two of these three are in place then you are probably close to settling the matter and breaking the fast.

Easy Does It

Let's assume your fast has been for twelve hours or longer. How do you go about breaking it? You most definitely don't want to begin with solid food. You start with fluids, which will settle in your stomach and begin the process of awakening the digestive fluids and tract. Even if you have fasted for just one day, I would still suggest that you break your fast with liquids first.

It is best to choose natural juices that are more alkaline. The digestive juices in the stomach and intestine will need time to begin to secrete again. The cocktail needs time to reconstitute. Gastric acid and pancreatic enzymes, especially, are not readily available to assist the digestive process. These need to be restored. Likewise, your saliva ducts will also have fallen on bad times, and these glands will need to kick into overdrive again. These things take time, so the early intake of liquids and even light solids will not be met with a fully functioning stomach.

Opinion varies on what is ideal to wake up the stomach, but the general view is that initially the juices should be light, not a fruit pulp, but full of natural sugar (fructose). You want to give your body a good reason to awaken. My favorite is apple juice made from concentrate. It is inexpensive, full of nourishment and fructose, and light in constitution. Fruit juices that have the highest water content, like watermelon, are the easiest to digest. But you could use a variety of strained juices, such as grape or pear. Some recommend tomato. Don't use citrus juices like grapefruit, orange, and lime, as these don't have the more alkaline pH balance.

Some would contend that you should also take into account your blood type, as this will dictate whether you have an acidic or alkaline stomach. For those of blood group O, being on the acidic end, less acidic fruit juices would be best; but the A's would do well with more acidic citrus juices in due course. [1] I'm not suggesting that you do a blood test before fasting, but when and if you do learn about your blood type this could be a helpful guide. If you have questions, seek professional advice.

---

1   Peter J. D'Adamo, *Eat Right 4 Your Type: The Individualized Diet Solution to Staying Healthy, Living Longer and Achieving Your Ideal Weight: 4 Blood Types, 4 Diets* (New York: Putnam, 1996).

To break the fast, sip a small glass of your chosen juice. On a shorter fast you might sip the juice over the course of an hour, and then crave something more. If you have been on an extended fast this is less likely. It will perhaps be several hours before you are ready for another, which you sip slowly over the course of a few hours. Don't forget to continue drinking water while you are doing this. You must maintain the intake of fluids.

When you are ready for something more, you may want to try a light consommé type of soup. My personal preference is a light beef broth. Don't choose a thick or spicy soup, which would cause such an assault on your taste buds that it would feel like you were burning your mouth, and then the food would sit like a lump in your stomach. Drink a glass of water about an hour before eating, but don't drink a lot with the soup.

If you have done a shorter fast, you might feel ready for a light soup three or four hours after your glass of juice. When breaking an extended fast, I wouldn't expect you to be ready for this until twenty-four hours after your first juice. The principle is that you are continuing to stay with liquids, but moving to more savory food. But be careful about the salt. And don't add condiments, even though you will probably be tempted to do so. If your body is reacting well to the initial juices, go for a light soup: hot is better, but no bread.

Having taken some juice, some suggest it is very healthful to eat some yogurt, but without fruit or additives. Although I have not done this myself, I believe it could be helpful. Be guided by what your body tells you it needs.

At this point most people take their first dose of caffeine again. But my caution to you would be to ensure it is very weak and contains very little milk. Avoid slipping into any of your old addictions.

Graduating to Solid Food

Liquids are the easy part of breaking a fast. You do this for the first day or so. What you are actually doing is waking up your stomach; don't expect much nourishment from these early drinks. Now you need to choose what solid food you are going to eat.

You need to continue to gradually build up your eating. Perhaps you can move toward a more solid soup, such as minestrone, vegetable, or heavy broth. Chew it thoroughly, as this will likely be the first time you sense that your saliva glands are waking. For an extended fast, start with only a small portion.

If your fast has been shorter you will be able to handle solid foods more quickly. Within four hours of breaking a one-day fast you may be able to handle something very light, a small portion. After eight hours you may find yourself ready for something more solid. Listen to your body and be gentle with it.

Twenty-four hours after a twenty-four-hour fast, the period of breaking your fast will be complete. A three-day fast will take longer. A seven-day fast will take perhaps five days, and longer fasts will take up to eight days. Be willing to treat this as part of the discipline of your fast.

As a guideline, don't give in to the temptation to eat a chocolate bar or other sweets at first. Your stomach will not be ready for them, and you could have very uncomfortable side effects. Remember that it takes up to several days for your stomach and digestive tract to reconstitute the digestive fluids and gain the right pH balance to begin the digestive process.

Reawakening Your Digestive System

By taking your first nourishment you are calling your digestive system to life again. Eating will feel good, every taste memorable. You can feel your body getting warmer and stronger as you begin to eat. You can sense new waves of energy. You will feel like you could run for miles. Your senses feel even sharper, if that were possible. Your sense of taste especially awakens, as you burst with the flavors and sensations in your mouth.

Blood forms an important part of the digestive process. When you begin eating it will again rush to the stomach, so you will need to rest and let your stomach do its work. Don't overeat or eat too soon, as this can cause light-headedness, dizziness, and nausea. You will notice that your body temperature will begin to rise almost instantly when you begin to eat some solid foods.

If you have been on an extended fast, the liquids, with their nourishment, will run through you like a bath with no plug. Over the next few days you will have your first solid bowel movement, which will probably be painful as the bowel reopens. If you begin eating too much too soon, or eat the wrong foods too quickly, you will suffer severely. Part of the discipline of your fast is to be a wise steward of your body as you break the fast.

On one occasion I stayed on a fast too long and only had three or four days to break the lengthy fast before important social commitments, including meals, became unavoidable. I had a real sense that the Holy Spirit was aiding my body, and I was eating normally on the fourth day without any pain or side effects. But you must never presume on this, unless it is very clear to you that God is helping you in this way.

Your bad breath will normally last about a week. You will suddenly realize that it is gone. But don't breathe in someone's face to check!

Shaking Off the Death and Darkness

During a fast death can often hang over you, in the sense that you are inviting death by not eating. In a journal entry toward the end of a fast in 1993, I wrote about "the monotony of this monochrome existence (e.g., no food)—forever black and white. No life. Just life and death together in me. The more I give life during my fast the more I touch into the death. Is this to be the way for all of my life?"

From the moment you decide to break the fast you must begin declaring that you want the restoration of life, not death. Your spirit must begin to feed upon the Lord in this way. Food is life for your body; the love of God is life for your spirit. After an extended fast you can feel like it is still there—lingering, refusing to leave until you tell it to do so.

The discipline it takes to break the fast will wipe you out if you aren't wiped out already. Don't be surprised if you go into a time of real depression. See this phase as an opportunity to engage the darkness for the last time as you let it go. You must give all of this to the Lord. This experience alone can be quite heavy.

You will see more clearly the darkness and anguish that you were under. Some start to see the death accompanying fasting for the first time. If you are in that category, talk to someone. Ask for help if you need it, as it is often through your relationship with others that you are able to see the Lord. Invite the Lord to lift the suffering.

Some people find the aftershock very severe. You were bringing a lot of death into your spirit while fasting; so after beginning to break the fast you may find it hard to shake off the death feelings. Some also have difficulty starting to eat again. The idea of eating might even make you feel sick.

Because many people carry a lot of self-hate, beating up their body through fasting suits them well. Returning to normal eating means they will need to let go of the hate so they can be at peace with their bodies. A great deal of self-cleansing often accompanies fasting. Note it and welcome it.

You may discover that you have a fear of putting food in your stomach. Or you may have a problem being nice to yourself after a period of punishing yourself. All of these are things to work through to get back to "normal."

Ironically, for the first week after breaking an extended fast you may feel like you are still losing weight. Though your stomach is not fully functioning yet, you probably will be. And if you are disciplined to break the fast slowly you won't be eating enough to maintain your weight. Make a note of this so that you will know for future fasts. Waking your body from this slumber is a delicate operation; so remind yourself and others that you aren't yet ready for a three-course meal.

Continue writing notes in your journal as if you are still on the fast. Keep a record of what you are experiencing. Monitor the spiritual world, since much knowledge will often be released to you during these times. During the fast, especially an extended one, you may have become quite envious of those who were freely eating—enjoying the comfortable life you could not enjoy. You will need to confess this to the Lord as well.

Finally, be very aware of the onset of pride. Doing an extended fast can feed one's pride. You may discover that your weight loss and new sense of health and vitality gives you opportunity to boast. Honor God, not men. Don't find yourself under the accusation of Christ against the Pharisees. Remember that this was an act of obedience, nothing more. Humble yourself, and keep the spirit of the surrender of the fast.

Changing Your Lifestyle

After an extended water-only fast, you will likely feel a need to review your normal eating habits. While you are gradually breaking your fast is the best time to make substantial changes.

Eat fresh and healthy. Go organic if you can. Avoid salt, unhealthy fats, processed foods, fried foods, foods that are high in cholesterol, and foods that you have been addicted to in the past. This is your big chance: don't go back there. This can be part of a new balance in your relationship with your body—an ongoing benefit from the fast.

Look especially at the caffeine you consume, particularly via coffee and tea. Unfortunately there is not always an available substitute in Western social life for these drinks, apart from water and sugary drinks. But you will traumatize your body with caffeine overdose if you start taking it too soon. After an extended fast, eliminate caffeine for at least ten days—if you must return to it at all. You are also likely to hate water (and mints) for some time! Fortunately, you have the option of buying juices and decaffeinated coffee and tea.

One of the challenges of a water-only fast is that we can put on weight quickly in the month or two following the fast. Weight can be replaced by the body at an alarming rate. We can find ourselves back up to our normal (unhealthy?) weight before we know it. For some of us it will take more discipline to avoid this happening than it took for us to fast.

The key is to capitalize on the fast as we break it. We have to see all the negative side effects that accompany fasting alongside the long-term benefits of allowing the body to shake off all the stored toxins that go with the overweight and obesity issues surrounding our lifestyle. Think this through very carefully and make some right decisions that honor you and the Lord.

CONCLUSION

Over the course of your fasting journey
you will build your own record of the
remarkable interventions of the Lord as
a result of your fasting journey. As an
encouragement in the meantime, here
are some of mine.

CELEBRATING VICTORIES: THE FRUIT OF FASTING

When my editor began reading the text of this book he was surprised by the numerous references to death. This was not a coincidence, but rather a reflection of what fasting has been to me: feeling death, entering the death of Christ, or simply wanting to die because it was all getting to be too much. I'm glad this was pointed out to me, though, because I don't want to leave this as the last impression. Unlike others who have had victorious encounters with Christ while fasting, for me the joy of fasting comes as a result of engaging death and being privileged to stand with Christ and make a difference in the Kingdom of God. But this is what happens *after* a fast—sometimes long after.

So the enduring memory of most of my extended fasts has been twofold: on the one hand the darkness of the period of fasting and on the other hand the profound significance of the changes wrought by the fast and its fruit. In my fasting I have touched into my own death while seeing chains broken in other people's lives when the knowledge I had gained has been applied. Likewise, seeing my life and my fasting as intercession has meant I have been able to bring to others what I would not otherwise have been able to share.

If I were to select the one spiritual discipline that has contributed most to my deepening walk with Christ, it would have to be fasting. One of the enduring lessons of fasting has been my realization that in our Christian life two extremes walk hand in hand: life and death. Christ gave life by enduring the death of the Cross so that we never have to go there ourselves. But He also called us to death (see 1 Corinthians 15:31), while telling us that we will have joy (see John 16:24).

Those of us in the Western church are in danger of wanting the life of Christ with all its joy and triumphs but without the death of the Cross.[1] One obvious sign of spiritual maturity is knowing the balance of both death and life in Christ. The joy comes later, but is enduring.

The two things that seem very true: if, on the one hand, I fast for twenty days, then I can enjoy the rest of the year without repeating this denial! Likewise, the joy endures forever, while the pain is but for a short season.

Fasting Out of Obedience

One of my most difficult fasts took place one February when I fasted for no other reason than that the Lord required it. I had no specific reason to fast, and I had previously learned that the dead of winter in the UK was not the time to do a water-only fast. But the Lord clearly told me to do so, so I obeyed. I didn't know how long the fast would last as I began.

---

2 For more on this subject see Frances M. Young, *Brokenness and Blessing: Towards a Biblical Spirituality* (London: Darton, Longman and Todd, 2007).

The temperature outside was nearing twenty degrees below zero, and the fast was a killer. After the first day my body was exceptionally cold and ached all the time. I spent most evenings in a steaming bath or a warm bed. But at the end of five days the Lord said to me, "Well done." That was it! No other fruit from the fast—no breakthroughs, no special anointing or knowledge. This was simply an act of obedience on my part.

I knew God was testing me, reminding me that Jesus led His disciples into a storm (see Matthew 8:23–27) and that if He chose to do something similar to me then I should shut up and obey Him! Reflecting on this fast many years later I realized that the Lord was testing me for bigger things to come, to see whether I would act faithfully on what I heard—without moaning and questioning.

Fasting has been part of my personal journey for almost fifty years. Looking back I can see that it has both helped define the direction of my life and reinforce positive change. To talk in detail of all of these experiences would take more than a short chapter, but what I would like to do is mention some of them and highlight in retrospect what they actually did to help define who I have become and am becoming.

By sharing my journey I am not trying to communicate that this is the way others should live. It is one of the most brutal and grueling paths I can imagine, but it is also one of the most rewarding. So I am careful, for instance, to avoid intimating that it is a way to get rich quick or a fast-track highway to super-sainthood. This is far from the case. It is a discipline, rather, that involves the whole of one's person, and that helps define who we are and how far we are willing to go for Christ and for our beliefs.

In outlining some of my battles and outcomes, then, I am not suggesting that I have in any way arrived spiritually. Far from it—just ask my wife and closest friends! Instead, I mention these experiences in order to identify the range of ways that fasting can be used to break glass ceilings, breach thick walls, and shake off bad times. I will begin with the most common one in my life: seeking the Lord for knowledge to change an intractable situation.

Fasting for Spiritual Knowledge

I have had a longstanding interest in why people fail to find intimacy with Christ and why people get emotionally ill. Although these are not automatically connected, both require personal change to resolve, and both are able to be resolved to some degree with the Lord's help.[2]

By the 1970s I had begun to see patterns in my lay pastoral work with people, noting the kinds of things they needed to do in order to work through deep problems in their lives. So when a person came to me for assistance I would help him or her as best I could, based on the knowledge and experience I already had. But at times I found myself unable to make suggestions for a way forward. In some of these cases I would fast for such a way. I always did this without telling the person what I was doing; I merely said that I would pray about the situation and see what the Lord said.

Most of the time I would be seeking knowledge for others, though on occasion I would need wisdom and guidance for myself. I discovered that during such fasts the Lord would give me a key that would help the person forward. After I had been given His answer I would then wait for the right moment to share it with the individual. I have learned that having some wisdom for a person does not automatically grant permission to declare it. Communicating the knowledge to the person is a separate step.

But when I would share my insights I would also teach the person how to apply them clinically, if appropriate. I have done this many times,

---

1   For more on these two topics see my book *Becoming More Human: Exploring the Interface of Spirituality, Discipleship and Therapeutic Faith Community* (Bletchley, Milton Keynes, UK: Paternoster, 2005).

helping numerous people find a way forward in their lives as a result. Over the last forty years I have had to do this less and less as I have developed sort of a "healing IQ" in regard to the disorders in people's lives and the way the Lord might tackle the problem. Having said that, though, each person is unique, so one should never assume that what worked for one person will also work for another.

An example of this type of fast occurred in 1993 when I was trying to resolve the question of the makeup of human nature. This was important for a particular person, as I had not been unable to help him resolve an issue despite my best efforts. Though the situation focused on this individual's physical ill health, my instinct was that it had a spiritual root. But since I couldn't get specific discernment on this, I fasted for him.

I had struggled for many years to try to describe human nature in a biblical way, but I couldn't find a rationale with which I was comfortable. This is what I wrote in my journal toward the end of this fast: "Did a study on 1 Corinthians 11:27–34. What a dynamic passage! Never before had seen inner healing in this biblical perspective. Here we see the roots of physical disorder being in the spirit. No healing without the Atonement. So good of the Lord to show me new truth."

This meditation led me to the idea of the unity of body and spirit, which I subsequently rediscovered in the first three chapters of Genesis. Over the following years I began to develop these concepts, seeing in them an elegantly simple Hebrew idea. This allowed me to avoid the minefield of Greek bipartite or tripartite thinking and gave me a way forward to talk about a spiritual model of human makeup. I subsequently began to apply the principle that the human spirit can condition our physical makeup while our physical condition can impact our spirit.

Fasting as Part of Surrendering to Christ

Some dark aspects of my nature have been confronted through fasting. For example, at one point I had resisted for several months to act in obedience to the Lord because I refused to share with people what the Lord had revealed to me. I knew that if I did what the Lord had asked of me it would change the direction of my life. My diary records: "I can only offer all this up to the Lord, together with my old, broken, damaged body, and plead for the mercy of God for my disobedience. Is it redeemable at this late hour?"

I was in my forties at the time, and it was while I was fasting that I made the decision to surrender to Christ and to act as He desired. A month later, while recovering from the fast, I did what He wished. This period was a tipping point in my life, as it began a journey that I am still enjoying some twenty years later.

At several points in my walk with Christ I have had to take major steps to surrender to Him. One time I had to lay down spiritual gifting for several years while He schooled me. On another occasion I was unable to do what He desired because of the obstruction of others. All such moments were accompanied by a season of fasting as I coped with what was being asked of me.

As a more recent example of surrender, in 2006 the Lord invited me to go and apologize to several local Christian leaders about the mistakes we made in the early years of planting Christ Church. He did not tell me, but rather asked me, to do this. It was something He recommended that I do. I was to do this without talking to others and only speak about it in our local congregation as and when it was appropriate and after I had completed the bulk of the task.

I visited these leaders over the course of several months. It was very hard, but confession is a key part of my ministry. I have even had to get accustomed to apologizing when I had little or no part in the original actions or the subsequent harm, which is never easy.

But fasting unto the Lord, in a sense, is always surrender to Christ. By the very act of self-denial we are saying that we are putting Him first, that nothing else really matters. His perspective is what we choose as well. His wishes become our wishes, His death is our death, His pain is our pain.

I have often thought, while fasting, that it is probably the closest a healthy, free person will ever come to a "living death." Although I have had several near-death experiences in my life, it is fasting that takes me to the place of connecting with the sufferings of Christ. But this is the diametric opposite of one issue I have tackled through fasting: the problem of gluttony.

Fasting to Break Gluttony

On a couple of occasions I have used fasting to break personal gluttony. Not that I am a compulsive glutton, but at times I have found myself in a place where the regular routine of eating has become so presumed that I believe it is no longer by grace but my right.

Although I would not recommend fasting as a way for everyone to break an eating habit, it has been appropriate for me. For most people it is much easier to discipline their eating than to go on a fast. But in practice this may not always be as easy as it sounds. It has not been for me. Let me give you an example.

My wife and I were living on a beautiful lake in Starnberg, just outside Munich, in southern Germany. The Eastern Bloc of communism still existed and Mary and I were working with a mission smuggling Bibles into these closed countries. Let my journal explain: "All those breads, cheeses, cold meats, and the good company of Mary and Steve to enjoy it with every day . . . I have lost control of my eating. It's a comfort gone too far for me. I have known for some time that I am putting on weight. I have stopped doing my exercise program. I have really lost it. This fast is about bringing my body back under control. I must break the body's gluttony—remind it who is in charge."

Bringing the body into submission in this way is a basic need for all of us at one time or another. We eat more food than our bodies need, we refuse to exercise, and we eat the wrong foods for our health. The Western world has seen a dramatic rise in the number of people who are overweight. The Centers for Disease Control and Prevention has found that 34 percent of adults aged twenty and over in the United States are obese.[3]

Going on a fast can be the first step to changing our lifestyle. When I'm fasting I try to focus on spiritual realities, which are beyond life here and the meeting of my physical needs. Human appetites can take over—becoming all consuming, and becoming the end-all of our lives. We begin thinking no further than the next meal or the next beverage. We become enslaved to our appetites.

During another fast I wrote in my journal that I no longer felt "trapped in my body." Over time I had noticed that I had become more and more driven by my body's physical appetites; my life focused around them. If we aren't careful, the pampering of our bodies through food and drink can become the very center of our lives. At such times I have needed to refocus my life on eternal things: Christ, my destiny in Him, helping to hasten His return, fulfilling my call, and so on. Fasting can be a useful tool in achieving this.

On one particular fast there was a tipping point where I was beginning to break the demands of the body's physical needs. By fasting I

2   "New CDC Study Finds No Increase in Obesity Among Adults; But Levels Still High," National Center for Health Statistics, U.S. Department of Health and Human Services, Hyattsville, MD, November 28, 2007, http://www.cdc.gov/nchs/pressroom/07newsreleases/obesity.htm.

returned my focus toward Jesus. Knowing Christ in this way has been a longtime, conscious intent in my life, and I know when I have lost this focus. But my body has not been the only thing that has on occasion needed refocusing. At times my future has been in the balance.

Fasting at Defining Moments

Fasting has played a key role in helping me find direction and definition. I have been aware of the link between self-denial, surrender, and a change of direction in my life.

One time as I went into a fast I wrote in my journal, "It is going to hurt. I have never done a fast in January. Well, here goes. This is a downhill toboggan, a wild roller coaster, a step of faith into the darkness. Feels like a darkness around the Throne that I must enter and go through before I can see and meet the Lord and sit at His feet. But I fear this fast for the cold, the loneliness, and the pain."

This twenty-one-day fast in the depth of winter was one of the most difficult and seemingly foolhardy fasts I've ever done. But it was an act of obedience, and it became one of the defining seasons of my life. It concluded with my moving out of London to a different part of England, setting up a new business, then later birthing Christ Church Deal (CCD), the *Rapha* journey, the Life Giving Trust, and a lot of books and teaching.

At times I would go into a fast knowing what would happen, while at other times I would be fasting for something quite different when another focus would begin to emerge. On one occasion I had completed a fast before I realized what had happened, what the Lord had done in answering another prayer of mine that I had not put on the original agenda.

I stopped another fast when I found the Lord giving me something that I had not gone into the fast seeking. On this occasion the outcome was also a blessing for my wife, Mary, and my son, Christopher. Let me explain.

Fasting in Times of Despair

It was 1990. I was the managing director of several successful property companies based in London. But then we had the UK property crash, engineered by Prime Minister Margaret Thatcher as a means of deflating an inflationary economy. One minute interest rates were low, the next they were 17.5 percent. Within a few weeks Mary and I found ourselves half a million dollars in debt. We lost everything: the businesses, our hopes and dreams, and even our home. We were devastated.

I went down to the local job center to seek dole money and a housing benefit so that we could rent a place to stay, as we had no money. Before moving out of our home Mary went to bed for a week and, understandably, did not want to get up. I was so low that I contemplated taking my own life. If it were not for those I loved, I probably would have done so.

I was in such a rage against God and the world that I realized I was capable of anything. I knew I needed to fast to make sense of the loss of the last ten years of my life, which was the way I saw things at the time. Let me quote my journal: "In the last few days I have found myself hating people who have routines. I hate the rich. I hate those who have not been through what I have been through. I have no job, no money, no income, no security, no routines, no future, nothing to work for. I find such anger and jealousy flowing out of me when I am alone, mostly driving. Look at all the well-appointed retirees, all those who do not have to labor for nothing—to fill a purse with holes. I guess I have felt this way for some time, but in the sixth day of this fast, in my weakened state, I am more able to admit it. I cannot pretend anymore. This did not used to be me, Lord. I've lost it completely. God, redeem me, before my friends and the watching world . . . now. For I have no help but You."

At the end of the fast I went through a time of deep spiritual renewal. The day after I broke the fast I wrote in my journal, "At the morning worship I felt my anointing return—waves of deep passion from the heart of God for people's healing. The passage, sermon, and worship all fit this theme. Remarkable. I felt the Lord giving me back His Spirit for the church. In your time, O Lord, in your good time."

I know that had I not fasted I would have been unable to recover from losing all I owned. Looking back I now realize that God had me in His school of despairing brokenness, and I was unwilling to graduate the way He needed me to.

Provision has always been a battle for me; so fasting has been my lot on numerous occasions.

Fasting for Provision

Some four years later, in 1994, I was fasting for provision to finance a business venture. Several of us felt this was what the Lord was going to do with our lives. But things were in a bad place; we were not seeing enough money come in each month to meet our expenses. But we saw remarkable provision that allowed us to stay afloat.

On another occasion when I was fasting for provision I learned, on the fourteenth day of the fast, that I was able to sell an apartment I owned in one of the companies. This released some eighty thousand dollars. We also won a Pre-Investment Feasibility Study (PIFS) contract worth about the same. A good start. Other things followed and it began to look like a formidable list of provision, so I felt able to break the fast.

Another time we had ordered steel for a very important fabrication job, but it was delayed. When we fasted together as a team, the problem was suddenly no longer there. The steel was delivered.

I have never kept a record of how much I have seen come in as a result of fasting, but it has certainly been hundreds of thousands of dollars for the businesses and the Lord. Having said that, though, this has never been a magic formula. In fact, I would call it "blood money": money earned by Christ's blood, my own, and sometimes that of others. So please do not see fasting as a get-rich-quick formula.

For me, one of the golden rules in seeking the Lord for this kind of provision is that He is already affirming through others that this is right, that He is waiting on our obedience to honor us. It is never wise to fast for provision unless God has first taken the initiative to invite you to do so, together with the confirmation of others.

Fasting for Renewal or Resolution

The fast that brought about the significant financial provision through the sale of the apartment and the PIFS contract was also undertaken for another reason. It was a fast for provision, but it also had a much more personal aspect to it. As I wrote in my journal, "I am at a total and utter end of myself. I cannot ever recall feeling this way before. I need to break this fast. I have had headaches for several weeks. I feel I want to lie down somewhere and die. Can God really mean that all His promises, hopes, and plans should end like this?"

This was another one of those times of absolute despair. In writing this book I found myself back there, struggling with the devastating exhaustion and confusion. I was in such a dark place after believing I was following Christ in these business ventures. I had wrongly assumed they would succeed. Yes, Christ was in the ventures, but I had to learn that He had very different purposes than those I had assumed.

This was one of those instances when I gently moved out of the darkness during the fast. I was able to allow the Lord to heal my spirit by His having to bear up my body while I fasted. It may sound like a contradiction, but in some of my fasts, like this one, my spirit grew stronger as my body grew weaker. This strength did not necessarily bring with it a sense of God's presence, but it brought a sense of His strength.

Also, by not eating I was able to focus on what was really important—Christ and my calling. Fasting took me back to basics. I was able to remind myself of what was really important, what was eternal, and what I could let go of, at least for a season. The tyranny of the tiredness was able to fall away as I focused again on Christ. I could give all these other things to Him because in my weak and fragile state I could carry none of it.

The other outcome of this fast, as in others, was that when I began to break the fast and focus again on Christ and my future I was quickly strengthened in body. All the problems with which I went into the fast were beginning to break free. But it was also a time of renewal of focus on Christ and His purposes rather than so much on immediate circumstances. In short, it set me again on my destiny, not the seductive alluring of the drive to "succeed"—even if I believed I was succeeding for Jesus!

While the goal of some of my fasts has simply been to see the exhaustion and tyranny of life broken so that I could refocus my life, the clear purpose of other fasts has been to stand with Christ in order to see Him step into a situation and resolve it. Most of us, at one time or another, will need such resolution in our lives, and fasting can help this happen. Let me illustrate.

We wanted to plant a church on the Downham Estate in Lewisham, in southeast London. It was a large housing estate that had very little Christian witness at the time. We needed a building in which to meet. We sensed that only Christ could resolve this. So we prayer-walked the streets and also held a fast, inviting the Lord to step in. He did: a local school welcomed us after initially saying no.

We were, in a sense, taking the ground for the Lord and beginning to raise a standard for Him. This was a corporate act, as a number of us stood together in this. It is so good when you have a sense that the Lord is going before you and things are happening the way you feel they should.

Discovering My Life Destiny

I have been a follower of Christ since the early 1960s. I have lived a full and active life in Christian service and in the business world. Although I don't see these two roles as distinct or mutually exclusive, I am aware that many people do.

I have done a lot in my lifetime, including earning, losing, or giving away a lot of money—channeling significant amounts into missions, especially church planting. I have also visited over seventy countries around the world, preaching on every continent except South America. I have felt the pleasure of the Lord on all of this. But that was just my apprenticeship. He has been keeping me occupied while making other plans for me. What I thought was the end purpose for my calling was merely kindergarten.

When I was still in my teens I was given a prophetic word that I have never forgotten: "Remember, Peter, it takes fifty years for a young oak tree to produce its first acorn." I was never sure that was true, but I kept it in mind through a note in one of my old Bibles.

Then in 1996 when we lost our trading advantage with a new product that we were bringing to the market through a business I was helping to birth, I found myself very broke and having nothing to do. So Susan Williams and I, with the support of my wife, Mary, began running wholeness weekend workshops, as well as being cofounders of Christ Church Deal. During this time I became very aware that all the years of fasting and seeking the Lord for myself and for others was beginning to reap a significant harvest. I realized that I was just beginning my real ministry.

I had always preferred to lead from the back. I have never been comfortable as a leader out in front and in the limelight. I am more at ease in one-on-one relationships, listening to people's pain and seeing others succeed. So this shift was going to be particularly difficult for me, as I was aware that things were about to change and I would be expected to lead from the front from now on.

For most of my life I have sensed a Levitical call from the Lord. The Levites were in a sense the "business managers" of the priestly tribe of Levi, handling all practical functions (see 1 Chronicles 9:14–34; 15:1–16:6; 23:1–32; 26:20). Their bloodline was set aside for special purification, cleansing, and dedication to God's purposes (see Numbers 8:5–26). Levites were not allowed personal ownership of land; instead they were given a privileged position in forty-eight Levitical towns, together with the pasturelands around them, as their perpetual possession (see Leviticus 25:32–34; Numbers 18:20; Joshua 21:41). It has taken many years for me to begin to fulfill this call in the way I believe God requires.

Connected to this, in 1994 the Lord began talking to me about my future. In April of 1995 He prompted me to consider 2 Chronicles 14 to 16, the story of Asa, king of Judah. The king's arrogance in his old age eventually forced the Lord to take his life. God spoke to me with great force: *Peter, remember King Asa of Judah.* I understood immediately what He was saying. To help remind me of the importance of this word I had a piece of hand-sewn embroidery made by a friend in Vienna, Brenda Babcock. I now have these words hanging over the fireplace in my study as a reminder that the Lord is not yet finished with me. Neither will He allow me to wander from the unique destiny He has for me.

An Invitation

The examples I've shared help demonstrate how the Lord has used the spiritual discipline of fasting in my life. I have no doubt that much has been achieved through this grueling journey that wouldn't otherwise have been possible.

Now I'd like to invite you to begin, or continue, your own exploration of this discipline. Such a commitment is not to be taken lightly. It is holy ground, and you should have the Lord's invitation and permission. Let Him grow the urge in you.

If in doubt, begin very gently with short and simple fasts, perhaps with fasts that don't even involve abstaining from food. Begin keeping a journal about how the Lord is taking you on this journey. You will discover much about yourself, about others, and about Him. Even in the darkest moments He never fails, for He is our God and Master.

Appendix

THE EARLY CHURCH'S ATTITUDE TOWARD FASTING

The following is a summary of the early church's attitude toward fasting. Because it focuses more on a historical perspective than the actual practice of fasting, I have placed it here as an appendix. I hope those of you who are interested in this subject find it as informative as I did in writing it!

It is too simplistic to speak about Greek ideas (since there were so many of them!) as opposed to Hebrew/biblical ideas, but the early church[1] was profoundly influenced by the moral thought, medical understanding,

---

3   In referring to the "early church," I am not talking about believers in the New Testament period but rather in the first three centuries after that.

and anthropology within Greco-Roman society. Ideas related to fasting and asceticism were particularly impacted.[2]

The word "ascetic" derives from the Greek word *askesis*, which describes an athlete in training and all the accompanying disciplines. This word became a metaphor for rigorous dedication, hard work, and discipline to the point of self-denial. Such Greek attitudes shaped the Christian perception of the body back then, as well as the way we think about our bodies even today. [3] The champions of ascetic behavior in the early church were the Egyptian monks, both in their cenobitic (communal) and eremitic (solitary) forms.

Rather than abandoning fasting, as some suggest because of its relative absence in the New Testament, the early church took up this subject with almost too much vigor. One fourth-century source claimed, "Observe what fasting does: It heals diseases, dries up the bodily humors, casts out demons, chases away wicked thoughts, makes the mind clearer and the heart pure, sanctifies the body and places the person before the throne of God. . . . For fasting is the life of the angels, and the one who makes of it has angelic rank."[4]

Within both the Greco-Roman culture and the early church there was a contradiction or tension between the opposition of the body and the soul/spirit, on the one hand, and the practical recognition that the soul's condition and character are subject to bodily influences.[5] There was

---

2   For a balanced view of the way the early church emerged from its Judaic roots into the Greco-Roman *Pax Romano*, see Oskar Skarsaune, *In the Shadow of the Temple: Jewish Influences on Early Christianity* (Downers Grove, IL: Inter-Varsity, 2002).

3   For a response to the dualistic notion of love of spirit and hate of body, see P. Brown, *The Body and Society: Men, Women and Sexual Renunciation in Early Christianity* (New York: Cambridge University Press, 1988).

4   Teresa M. Shaw, *The Burden of the Flesh: Fasting and Sexuality in Early Christianity* (Minneapolis: Fortress Press, 1998), 1.

5   Ibid., 33.

also a separating or categorizing of the flesh-and-bones body from the soul, and in the process an elevation of the soul, following Greek ideas of human makeup. This in turn debased the body, another truly Greek idea.

The Greco-Roman philosophers, especially the Stoics, had a fundamental suspicion of the dangers of fleshly desire. They believed in the efficacy and purity of all that was spirit, but had an awareness that the flesh needed disciplining and controlling. On its own it would even stoop to the bestial.

The popularity of fasting in the early church was in part driven by a deep interest in the record of Adam and Eve in the Garden of Eden. Through such disciplines, Christians could align themselves with the Edenic ideal: a trouble-free place of humanity made in the image of God. This idyllic state is contrasted with what Basil of Caesarea described as the "fallen condition of humanity characterized by suffering, conflict, gender hierarchy, agricultural labor death [the curse found in Genesis 3 requiring man to labor and then die]. Fasting is a necessary way of repenting, and the image of the way of life in paradise."

Basil further noted that while humanity was created in the image and likeness of God, sinful action damaged the beauty of that image "by dragging down the soul toward passionate desires." All five senses are like open windows that need shutting in order to protect the soul and guard the body against the pollution of sensual pleasures. Fasting, like maintaining one's virginity for the Lord, adorns the body in order to please the Bridegroom.

In the idealized Eden humans ate only cereals and abstained from meat as well as sexual relations. Because they had profound intimacy with God, they already had everything they needed. The fall of man and woman ended this, but the picture of this ideal drove many in the early church to starve the body in order to exalt the soul. They had a desire to remove themselves from the moods and desires of the body, the "fallen" condition of humanity: from the worldly obsession with food, hunger, sex, fear, and death. In turning their attention away from these things they could begin to claim their original condition and intimacy with God.[6]

Part of what drove these ascetic attitudes was the fact that many in the Greco-Roman world considered gluttony the mother of all vice. By the fourth century major works were being written by Christians on the subject.[7] Gluttony was considered to be a psychological enemy that can be battled in part through physical methods. This led to a management of desire by diet, which many followed in both the regular fast days of the church, Tuesdays and Fridays each week, and the Lenten fast. In fact, F. J. Foakes-Jackson suggests that a variety of fast days were established to void pagan fasts, but with little conformity.[8]

The Didache is dated around sixty years after Christ and shows a solid commitment to fasting, "but not as the Jews." More potently, however, it fed the Christian ascetic movement itself, noting that a fat body cannot produce a clear or refined mind.[9]

Likewise, the "Shepherd of Hermes" linked fasting with the money one saves to give to the poor, and John Chrysostom stated that fasting without almsgiving was not fasting at all ("Homilies on Matthew," 77.6). Origen blessed those who fasted "to nourish the poor" ("Homilies on Leviticus," 10.2), while for Augustine fasting was avarice unless you gave away what you did not eat (Sermon 208).[10]

---

6   Ibid., 172.

7   For example, Evagrius of Pontus, "De vitiis quae opposita sunt virtutibus" ("In praise of the opposing virtue, abstinence," my translation), 2, PG 79, 1141A–B.

8   F. J. Foakes-Jackson, *The History of the Christian Church: From the Earliest Times to AD 461* (London: George Allen & Unwin, 1965), 584.

9   Shaw, *The Burden of the Flesh*, 88.

10   J. M. Nuth, "Fasting," in M. Downey (ed.), *The New Dictionary of Catholic Spirituality* (Collegeville, MN: Liturgical Press, 1993), 390–92.

But this interest in the desires of the flesh went much further. For us today it feels like it had a dark side. Teresa Shaw suggests that in the early church men's fear of women—the sexual power ascribed to her body and nature—drove the ascetic obliteration of female and made women second-class. Some women in the early church fasted to extremes, and also wore men's clothing, renouncing their womanhood and seeking to become like men. In some cases a woman's breasts shrank and she developed amenorrhea, the cessation of her monthly cycle. Such excess caused the "virgin to limp along . . . behind her male ascetic counterpart."[11]

Shaw notes that sexual and procreative desires were diminished by fasting, along with a woman making herself "appear masculine and stamp out the attraction of the female in her self-presentation towards earthly men."[12] Shaw also notes that almost all the evidence that we have of early fasting practices were from the hand of men; virtually none of her early sources were written by women.[13]

Conclusion

What becomes clearly evident in this brief outline is that the early church treated fasting very seriously. But many of these Christians took up a number of attitudes that were not so Christian, like a negative attitude toward their bodily appetites, a perspective that women are dangerous, and male domination of the church. Some of this extremism makes one cringe; so it is hoped that in this book we have struck something of an authentic biblical approach to the practice of fasting, together with the challenges, demands, and values of our own times.

---

11 Shaw, *The Burden of the Flesh*, 253.

12 Ibid., 246–50.

13 Ibid., 3.

BIBLIOGRAPHY

Brown, P. *The Body and Society: Men, Women and Sexual Renunciation in Early Christianity*. New York: Cambridge University Press, 1988.

Castelli, W. P., and G. C. Griffin. *The New Good Fat, Bad Fat: Lower Your Cholesterol and Reduce Your Odds of a Heart Attack*. Cambridge, MA: Fisher Books, 1997.

Colbert, D. *Toxic Relief: Restore Health and Energy Through Fasting and Detoxification*. Lake Mary, FL: Siloam Press, 2003.

———. *What Would Jesus Eat? The Ultimate Program for Eating Well, Feeling Great and Living Longer*. Nashville: Thomas Nelson, 2002.

D'Adamo, P. J. *Eat Right 4 Your Type: The Individualized Diet Solution to Staying Healthy, Living Longer and Achieving Your Ideal Weight: 4 Blood Types, 4 Diets*. New York: Putnam, 1996.

Hara, Y. *Green Tea: Health Benefits and Applications*. London: Marcel

Dekker, 2005.

Holmes, P. R. *Becoming More Human: Exploring the Interface of Spirituality, Discipleship and Therapeutic Faith Community.* Bletchley, Milton Keynes, UK: Paternoster, 2005.

————, *Trinity in Human Community: Exploring Congregational Life in the Image of the Social Trinity.* Bletchley, Milton Keynes, UK: Paternoster, 2006.

Holmes, P. R., and S. B. Williams. *Becoming More Like Christ: Introducing a Biblical Contemporary Journey.* Milton Keynes, UK: Paternoster, 2007.

————, *Changed Lives: Extraordinary Stories of Ordinary People.* Milton Keynes, UK: Authentic, 2005.

Hull, J. S. *Sweet Poison: How the World's Most Popular Artificial Sweetener Is Killing Us—My Story.* New York: New Horizon Press, 2000.

Nuth, J. M. "Fasting." In M. Downey (ed.), *The New Dictionary of Catholic Spirituality.* Collegeville, MN: Liturgical Press, 1993), 390-392.

Panksepp, J., and J. B. Panksepp. "The Seven Sins of Evolutionary Psychology." *Evolution and Cognition* 6, no. 2 (2000): 108-13.

Povey, R. *How to Keep Your Cholesterol in Check.* London: Sheldon Press, 1997.

Prince, D. *How to Fast Successfully.* Charlotte: Derek Prince Ministries, 1976.

————, *Shaping History Through Prayer and Fasting.* Charlotte: Derek Prince Ministries, 1973.

Rothenberg, F. S. "Fasting." In C. Brown (ed.), *The New International Dictionary of New Testament Theology*, vol. 1. Exeter, UK: Paternoster Press, 1971, 611–14.

Shaw, T. M. *The Burden of the Flesh: Fasting and Sexuality in Early Christianity.* Minneapolis: Fortress Press, 1998.

Skarsaune, O. *In the Shadow of the Temple: Jewish Influences on Early Christianity.* Downers Grove, IL: InterVarsity, 2002.

Staniforth, M. *Early Christian Writings: Apostolic Fathers.* London: Penguin, 1968.

Wallis, A. *God's Chosen Fast: A Spiritual and Practical Guide to Fasting.* Eastbourne, UK: Kingsway, 1982.

Wenger, P. "To humble" (semantic field 6700). In W. A. van Gemeren (ed.), *The New International Dictionary of Old Testament Theology and Exegesis*, vol. 3. Carlisle, UK: Paternoster, 1996, 451.

Williams, S. B., and P. R. Holmes. *Letting God Heal: From Emotional Illness to Wholeness.* Bletchley, UK: Authentic Media, 2004.